SOCIETY FOR OLD TESTAMENT STUDY
MONOGRAPH SERIES

GENERAL EDITOR
J. A. EMERTON

3

THE MEANING OF 'BĀMÂ' IN THE OLD TESTAMENT

A STUDY OF ETYMOLOGICAL, TEXTUAL AND ARCHAEOLOGICAL EVIDENCE

Other books in the series

R. N. WHYBRAY: *The Heavenly Counsellor in Isaiah xl 13–14: A study of the sources of the theology of Deutero-Isaiah.*

JOSEPH BLENKINSOPP: *Gibeon and Israel: The role of Gibeon and the Gibeonites in the political and religious history of early Israel.*

THE MEANING OF 'BĀMÂ' IN THE OLD TESTAMENT

A STUDY OF ETYMOLOGICAL, TEXTUAL AND ARCHAEOLOGICAL EVIDENCE

PATRICK H. VAUGHAN

Sometime Lecturer in the
Department of Religious Studies and Philosophy
Makerere University, Kampala

CAMBRIDGE UNIVERSITY PRESS

Published by the Syndics of the Cambridge University Press
Bentley House, 200 Euston Road, London NW1 2DB
American Branch: 32 East 57th Street, New York, N.Y.10022

Library of Congress Catalogue Card Number: 73-89004

ISBN: 0 521 20425 9

First published 1974

Printed in Great Britain
at the University Printing House, Cambridge
(Brooke Crutchley, University Printer)

CONTENTS

ACKNOWLEDGEMENTS

I should like to express grateful appreciation

to The Editorial Board of the Society for Old Testament Study's Monograph Series for accepting this volume for inclusion in the series;

to the Managers of the Hort Memorial Fund for a grant towards the cost of publication;

to Professor J. Weingreen, whose infectious delight in Biblical text and archaeology excited my interest in these subjects during student days in Trinity College, Dublin;

to Mr A. R. Millard, then Librarian of Tyndale House Library, Cambridge, who was my guide amongst the huge linguistic and archaeological resources of that library, and drew my attention to many works I should otherwise have missed;

to Professor J. A. Emerton, who made many valuable suggestions;

and to Hilary, my wife, for so understandingly granting 'leave of absence'.

PATRICK H. VAUGHAN
August 1973

ABBREVIATIONS

AASOR	*Annual of the American Schools of Oriental Research*
AI	R. de Vaux, *Ancient Israel* (London, 1961)
ANET	J. B. Pritchard (ed.), *Ancient Near Eastern Texts Relating to the Old Testament*^{2} (Princeton, 1955)
ARI	W. F. Albright, *Archaeology and the Religion of Israel*^{4} (Baltimore, 1956)
BA	*Biblical Archaeologist*
BASOR	*Bulletin of the American Schools of Oriental Research*
BDB	F. Brown, S. R. Driver, and C. A. Briggs (eds.), *A Hebrew and English Lexicon of the Old Testament* (Oxford, 1906)
BH	R. Kittel (ed.), *Biblia Hebraica*^{7} (Stuttgart, 1951)
BIES	*Bulletin of the Israel Exploration Society*
BSOAS	*Bulletin of the School of Oriental and African Studies*
CAD	I. J. Gelb, B. Landsberger *et al.*, *The Assyrian Dictionary of the Oriental Institute of the University of Chicago* (Chicago)
CTCA	A. Herdner, *Corpus des Tablettes en Cunéiformes Alphabétiques découvertes à Ras Shamra-Ugarit de 1929 à 1939* (Paris, 1963)
GK	E. Kautzsch (ed.), *Gesenius' Hebrew Grammar* (tr. A. E. Cowley)^{2} (Oxford, 1910)
HPAP	W. F. Albright, 'The High Place in Ancient Palestine', Supplement to *VT* IV (Leiden, 1957), pp. 242–58
ICC	*International Critical Commentary*
IEJ	*Israel Exploration Journal*
JBL	*Journal of Biblical Literature*
JPOS	*Journal of the Palestine Oriental Society*
KB^{1}	L. Koehler and W. Baumgartner (eds.), *Lexicon in Veteris Testamenti Libros* (Leiden, 1953)

KB^3	L. Koehler and W. Baumgartner (eds.), *Hebraïsches und Aramaïsches Lexikon zum Alten Testament* (Leiden, 1967), vol. I
LSJ	H. G. Liddell and R. Scott, *A Greek–English Lexicon*, revised H. S. Jones (Oxford, 1940)
LXX	Septuagint
MT	Massoretic Text
NEB	*New English Bible* (Oxford/Cambridge, 1970)
QDAP	*Quarterly of the Department of Antiquities in Palestine*
RB	*Revue Biblique*
RSV	Revised Standard Version
VT	*Vetus Testamentum*

NOTE

The forms *bāmâ* and *bāmôt* signify the Hebrew words בָּמָה and בָּמוֹת, and should be distinguished from bamah (pl. bamoth) which is used as the technical name for a cultic platform.

1(a). *Note the round, conical shape of the structure, the steps leading up to the flat top and the position inside enclosure walls (see p. 41).*

1(b). *The flight of steps leading up to the bamah. Note the building construction of loose, unhewn, field-stones, packed with smaller stones, and the general monumental scale of the structure (see p. 41).*

(*Photographs by the author.*)

2(a). *Part of the straight outer wall of the bamah, probably built in the reign of Jeroboam I. The stones in the centre of the picture are dressed in the style characteristic of the Israelite monarchy period (cf. pp. 47f.). The stones abutting the wall belong to later periods, and covered the original bamah.*

2(b). *The monumental flight of steps leading up to the bamah, probably built in the reign of Ahab (cf. p. 48).*

(Photographs by courtesy of the Israel Department of Antiquities and Museums.)

INTRODUCTION

In his prophecy against apostate Israelites, Ezekiel (xx 29) sarcastically puns on the meaning of the word *bāmâ*. 'What is the bamah', he asks, 'to which you come (*'attem habbā'îm*)?', suggesting that a bamah was a place or thing to which people 'come' – and what a worthless place to come to! The etymology is no doubt fanciful. It could hardly have been otherwise, since neither he nor his hearers were in a position to suggest any better etymology from their own language. But they did at least understand what he was referring to, since with their own eyes they had seen many a bamah. Even we moderns were in no position to improve on Ezekiel, having never seen a bamah (and so not knowing what it actually was), until recently when archaeologists claimed to have found remains of bamoth.

Naturally therefore some attempts were made to correlate these finds with the Biblical records and with the enigmatic word *bāmâ*. However, no very full treatment of the subject was given until that presented by W. F. Albright in his article 'The High Place in Ancient Palestine' (*Vetus Testamentum*, Supplement IV (1957)).[1] This article has subsequently come to be regarded by many as the *fons luminis* on the subject, and many of his conclusions have now found their way into the article on *bāmâ* in the third edition of Koehler/Baumgartner's *Lexicon* (1967).

It is unfortunate that Albright's presentation is vitiated by his theories of cults of the dead or hero-veneration in ancient Israel. Much of the evidence he gives for this is disputable, and one central point is no longer tenable. In addition, the progress of time has made further archaeological evidence available, which needs to be brought into discussion of the subject. The present monograph is an attempt to reconsider the whole question of the meanings of the word *bāmâ* as it is used in the Hebrew texts, and in particular to attempt a description of what a cultic bamah actually was.

CHAPTER I

THE DERIVATION OF THE WORD 'BĀMÂ'

There are many perplexities about the meaning and derivation of the word *bāmâ*. Of the 101 occurrences of the word in the Old Testament,[2] in over 80 cases it is a technical cultic term. It is a common word in the Deuteronomic editorial passages in Kings decrying the Baal cult, and carries a similar pejorative sense in Chronicles, Jeremiah, Ezekiel and other prophets. By contrast, the occurrences of the word in Samuel stand out, because *bāmâ* is there used in reference to the legitimate Yahweh cult.

The word is traditionally translated into English as 'high place'. But this translation is heavily dependent on the way in which the LXX understood *bāmâ*.[3] There is nothing in the word itself which gives any indication of its meaning, since no satisfactory derivation of the word can be found in Hebrew.

In the absence of any real evidence, it has been widely assumed until recently that *bāmâ* is derived from the supposed verbal root *bûm*,[4] on the same basis that the noun *qāmâ* is derived from the verbal root *qûm*. But such a verb is unknown, not only in Hebrew, but also in every other Semitic language.[5] It has therefore recently come to be realised that it is probably more satisfactory to regard *bāmâ* as being derived not from a verb at all, but from a (? pre-Semitic) noun,[6] since cognate nouns exist in Ugaritic, Akkadian, Moabite and possibly also Greek. However, with the lone exception of the word *bmt* in the Mesha Inscription, there is no extra-biblical occurrence of the word in a cultic sense. How the Hebrew word came to have this cultic sense has therefore long been an enigma.

Before discussing the Hebrew word *bāmâ*, it will be helpful to look at the cognate Ugaritic and Akkadian words, which throw light on the various derived meanings of the Hebrew word. We shall examine each in turn.

UGARITIC 'BMT'

The word *bmt* occurs seven times in Ugaritic literature to date. Till recently, it has been generally assumed that it means 'back'.[7] But M. Held[8] has argued that 'the meaning "back" hardly fits any of these passages'. After an examination of the contexts in which *bmt* occurs, Held proposes that the word most naturally means 'the middle of the body as a whole'. While it cannot be claimed that each individual passage irrefutably points to this meaning, the fact that two passages cannot bear the sense 'back' indicates that *bmt* must have a wider meaning than was previously supposed.

The clearest evidence that *bmt* cannot mean 'back' occurs in the description of El's mourning ritual on learning of Baal's death. Gashing his chin and cheek with a stone,

> he plows his chest like a garden
> harrows his *bmt* like a plain[9]
> (*yḥrṯ / kgn. 'ap lb.*
> *k'mq. yṯlṯ / bmt*).[10]

The physical action involved makes it plain that *bmt* cannot here mean 'back', while the synonymous parallel with 'chest' suggests a synonym such as 'ribs/sides'.

Anath's mourning for Baal is described in virtually identical wording,[11] and *bmt* must have the same meaning here also.[12]

Less clear is the description of Anath's single-handed fight against her enemies,

> she binds the heads to her *bmt*
> fastens the hands to her girdle
> (*'tkt / r'išt. lbmth.*
> *šnst / kpt. bḥbšh*).[13]

Precisely what manoeuvre is envisaged here is not quite clear, but the parallelism of *bmt* with *ḥbš* 'girdle' suggests that *bmt* may here mean 'waist' or 'side', rather than 'back'.

The above three occurrences of *bmt* refer to parts of the human anatomy; but from a further three passages, it is clear that *bmt* could be used of animals also. Thus as Ashera prepares for a journey, there is a detailed description of how Qadesh wa-Amrur secures the complicated saddle and harnessing apparatus, and then

> places Ashera on the donkey's *bmt*
> on the beautiful *bmt* of the jackass
> (*yštn.'aṯrt.lbmt.'r*
> *lysmsmt.bmt.pḥl*).[14]

In an identical formula, Paghat assists Daniel before a journey.[15] Although *bmt* is usually translated 'back' in both these cases, it could just as well refer to the whole trunk of the donkey's body (including its flanks) around which the elaborate trappings are fitted.

This possibility is strengthened by another occurrence of *bmt* (not mentioned by Held) in a tablet[16] which appears to be a delivery chit, listing, among other things, items for food including fat geese and oxen. Various cuts of beef are mentioned, including

> ten *bmt* of fat oxen
> (*'šr.bmt.'alp.mr'e*).

bmt will here refer to part of an ox's anatomy, possibly a whole carcase (i.e. the 'rib-cage'). It can hardly refer to the (exterior) 'back'.[17]

The seventh occurrence of *bmt* is usually taken to have an entirely different meaning. It occurs in the passage about the construction of the window for Baal's house. Baal then 'gives forth his holy voice... *bmt 'a*[....] *ṭṭṭn*,[18] Baal's enemies take to the woods'. The lacuna is commonly filled in to read *bmt 'arṣ*,[19] and translated 'the high places of the earth reel'. Thus Held confidently states, '*bmt* [*arṣ*] certainly denotes "the high places of the earth" and is to be equated with Akkadian *bāmāt šadî* on the one hand, and with Hebrew במתי ארץ on the other'. However, a good deal of caution needs to be exercised here, for such scanty evidence as there is in this damaged text does not rule out the possibility of *bmt* retaining its usual Ugaritic meaning here.[20] Our phrase may well be referring not to the effect of Baal's voice on the earth's surface, but to the bodily reactions of some of Baal's enemies, who are specifically mentioned in the next line.

Apart from one doubtful case, therefore, the seven Ugaritic occurrences of *bmt* suggest a meaning much wider than 'back';[21] something akin to the English word 'flank' would seem to cover all the human and animal contexts. As we shall see this is extraordinarily close to the meaning of Akkadian *bamtu*.

AKKADIAN 'BAMTU'

The word *bamtu* occurs frequently in Akkadian in anatomical contexts, and according to *CAD*[22] means 'chest, front of the chest'. It can be used either of human beings or animals. For instance in a medical text

> You put a bandage on the nape of his neck and on his chest [*pa-an-di-šu*];

or in an omen text

> If he cries 'Woe' during his sickness, lies on his chest (stomach) [*ban-ti-šu*], and does not turn over;

or in an El Amarna letter from Akko

> I prostrate myself seven times each, on the front [*pa-an-te-e*] and on the back.[23]

Examples of its use in relation to animals are

> If the malformed animal's ears are on the left side of its chest [*ba-an-ti*];

or from an extispicy text

If its thorax [*ba-am-tum*] is affected on the right side.

As will be seen from these examples, it is difficult to ascertain from the texts what precise part of the body is signified by *bamtu*. Help in this direction is, however, provided by the Sumerian vocabulary lists, with their Akkadian equivalents. In one of these, the Sumerian word UZU.TI.TI is explained by *bamtu*, but also by a second word *ṣēlu*, which means 'rib, side (part of the human and animal body)'.[24]

It seems therefore that *bamtu* is a rather general word, which we should avoid making too specific (as *CAD* does in its opening definition of 'chest, front of the chest'). The final discussion in the *CAD* article is clearer: 'The Sum. correspondences . . . as well as the Akk. refs. show that the word denotes the rib cage, the chest (as front of the human body), the thorax of an animal.' *bamtu* is thus very close in meaning to Ugaritic *bmt*. Much of what it signifies may be conveyed by the English word 'flank'.

AKKADIAN 'BAMÂTU'

The word *bamâtu* is classified by *CAD* (in contrast to von Soden)[25] as a homonym of *bamtu*, but one which occurs only in the plural. It is treated as a *plurale tantum* meaning 'open country, plain'. It only occurs in agricultural and military contexts, and obviously refers to a certain type of terrain.

Frequently it occurs as one element in the three-fold division of an area into city, cultivated land, and *bamâtu*. It would thus appear to signify the wild uncultivated land bordering on the cultivated fields which surround the city, as the following 'agricultural' texts (taken from the *CAD* article) suggest:

if a man (is bewitched) either in a field or outside (the city) or in the *bamâtu*;
(the waters) have carried off *bamâtu*, flooded the arable land;
bamâtu is being put in cultivation;
(the lamb) feeds on the grass in the *bamâtu*.

'Military' texts confirm *bamâtu* as one element in an identical three-fold division of land:

I spread the bodies of their warriors throughout the *bamâtu* of the mountains [*ba-ma-at šadî*], and around their cities;
I made (the blood of their warriors) flow over the lowland and the *bamâtu* in the mountains [*ba-ma-a-te ša šadî*];
I collected (the scattered army) from everywhere in the plain and in the *bamâtu*;
I dyed red the plain, the region outside the cities and all the *bamâtu*;
The lowlands of Tuplias, plain and *bamâtu*;
City and *bamâtu* will be plundered.

In the last group, *CAD* translates *bamâtu* as 'level ground'. But the expression 'level ground of the mountains' can clearly not be regarded as satisfactory sense. In any case the word occurs alongside 'plain (EDIN)', and thus will signify something more geographically distinct from plain than 'level ground'.

The evidence of these contexts suggests that *bamâtu* described open country which is (as it were by definition) uncultivated, yet could be used as pasture, or cultivated, and is frequently a scene of battle. Hilly slopes or foot-hills surrounding cities at once suggest themselves. (Since battles are not fought on rugged mountain heights, any sense of high mountain peaks or ridges must be dismissed.)

These translational problems pose the question whether *CAD* may not be mistaken in supposing that *bamâtu* 'must be assumed to be a *plurale tantum* and, therefore, is not connected with *bamtu* A ["half"] or *bamtu* B ["chest"]'. We have already seen that the basic idea signified by *bamtu* is connected with the rib-cage of humans and animals. Von Soden may be justified in treating *bamâtu* as the plural of *bamtu*, but occurring only in a specialised (topographical) context with the derived meaning 'hill-slopes'. For foot-hill terrain with low undulating ridges sloping up from a plain, looking like the flanks of giant beasts, might well be thought of as 'rib-cages of the mountains'.

Hebrew usage supports this. The Hebrew expression *bāmᵒṯê 'ereṣ* is generally accepted as being equivalent to Akkadian *bamât šadî*. But the Hebrew word *bāmᵒṯê* is used not only in topographical contexts but also anatomical ones. As will be discussed below, this is an indication that a single concept is being used in two contexts. It is likely that the same thing is happening with its Akkadian cognate.

THE APPARENT MEANINGS OF 'BĀMÂ' IN THE OLD TESTAMENT

We may begin by noting that there are two forms of the construct plural of *bāmâ* – *bāmôṯ* (the most common) and *bāmᵒṯê*.[26] The latter form is found exclusively in poetry, and only in one kind of context. This context is invariably one in which Yahweh either 'treads'[27] upon *bāmᵒṯê 'ereṣ* (or some other closely related phrase), or causes his favoured one (usually the king) to do so. The exact significance of these expressions is no doubt lost to us now; but it is clear that treading upon *bāmᵒṯê 'ereṣ* is essentially a divine activity, possible indicating ownership of the land.[28]

Expressions of this kind occur no fewer than twelve times,[29] suggesting that they are a stock poetic formula, probably very ancient. In each case there is no indication that the word *bāmᵒṯê* refers to any cultic object, for it invariably occurs in contexts which require an anatomical or topographical sense. This form of the word thus contrasts sharply with the form *bāmôṯ*, which invariably has a cultic sense. We shall examine each of these senses in turn.

i. bāmºṯê *with anatomical and topographical senses*

As already noted, the primary sense contained in the Ugaritic *bmt* and Akkadian *bamtu* is the concept of 'rib-cage', various contexts demanding slight variations in English translation (chest, side, flank, etc.). It needs to be stressed that there is no idea of *height* inherent in this concept at all.[30] Three passages in the Old Testament (each with the pleonastic plural) require an anatomical sense, and thus very clearly reflect the Ugaritic and Akkadian sense.

Deuteronomy xxxiii 29 is best translated:

> Your enemies shall come cringing to you,
> And you shall tread on their bodies/backs
> (*wᵉ'attâ 'al-bāmôṯêmô ṯiḏrōḵ*)

and not 'on their high places' as RSV and many others have rendered it.[31]

Similar will be the sense of the phrase

> *wᵉḏôrēḵ 'al-bāmºṯê yām*

in Job ix 8. *yām* without the article will here be a proper name – Yam,[32] the mythological serpent known to us through Ugaritic literature, who was conquered by Baal. The verse should therefore be translated:

> And who trampled the back of Yam.[33]

Again Isaiah xiv 14

> *'e'ᵉle 'al-bāmºṯê 'āḇ 'eddamme lᵉ'elyôn*

is best translated:

> I will rise upon the back[34] of a cloud,
> I will make myself like Elyon.

The RSV rendering 'I will ascend above the heights of the clouds' misses the true relationship between Elyon and the clouds. It is not that he dwells *above* the clouds, but (as other passages suggest) that he rides *upon* them.[35] *bāmᵒṯê* in this passage is particularly close to the sense of *bmt* in the two Ugaritic passages cited above where Ashera and Daniel are placed on the donkey's *bmt*. We may also note in passing that the idea of riding is not altogether absent from both Deuteronomy xxxiii 29 and Job ix 8 – placing one's feet on enemies' bodies probably implies that they are fit only to be used as humble steeds of the victor.

There remain nine passages where *bāmᵒṯê* occurs in a topographical context. It has been common practice to list these passages under a separate heading, and to assume that in them *bāmᵒṯê* has a different derived meaning, 'heights'.[36] But as the continuity of the phrase (notably with the accompanying verb *drk 'al* in both groups of passages) indicates, this is a distinction demanded by English usage only, and was not a distinction in the mind of the Hebrew writers.

It has already been suggested that the Akkadian plural noun *bamâtu* (especially in the phrase *bamât šadî*) must be related in some manner to the Hebrew phrase *bāmᵒṯê 'ereṣ*. But whereas in Akkadian the word seems to have been a mundane one used in prose to describe foot-hills, in Hebrew it is used only in poetic and (almost always) supernatural contexts.

Micah i 3 may be taken as typical:

> For behold, Yahweh is coming forth out of his place, and will come down and tread upon the 'flanks of the earth' (*wᵉyāraḏ wᵉḏārak 'al-bāmᵒṯê-'āreṣ*) and the mountains will melt.

If *CAD* is correct (and as indicated, there are reasons for questioning this) in supposing that *bamâtu* means 'level ground', this is certainly not a meaning which is appropriate in any of the Hebrew occurrences of the phrase *bāmᵒṯê 'ereṣ*.

The Hebrew phrase refers to some mythological mountains upon which Yahweh was visualised as walking, when he appeared in theophany.[37] But the word *bām^oṯê* itself does not contain the idea of mountains or heights. It still retains its fundamental anatomical sense of 'body, side, flank'. It is only the context – 'flanks *of the earth/land*' – which make it clear that mountains are being referred to.

With two exceptions, *bām^oṯê* with this topographical sense occurs only within the stock poetic formula about Yahweh treading/riding upon *bām^oṯê 'ereṣ*, or causing his favoured one to do so. The two exceptions are in David's Lament after Jonathan's death on the slopes of Gilboa (2 Samuel i 19 and 25), the full pathos of whose opening line now stands out strikingly:

> Thy glory, O Israel,
> is slain upon thy [mountain] slopes (*'al-bāmôṯêḵā*)

– a word evocative of precisely the location where Israel's glory proverbially expected to be vindicated! But more significantly for our purposes, these two verses indicate that early Hebrew did use *bām^oṯê* in a secular context – in this case a context identical with the Akkadian military texts.

ii. bāmâ = '*bamah*'

Everywhere else that *bāmâ* occurs in the Old Testament (apart from the two cases discussed in (v) below), it has a cultic sense. A typical instance is 1 Kings xiv 23:

> They also built for themselves *bāmôṯ* and *maṣṣēḇôṯ* and *'ᵃšērîm* on every high hill and under every green tree.

Here *bāmôṯ* is the technical term for one item among several of the cultic installations at the traditional shrines, and will refer to the man-made platforms which will be discussed in detail in the next two chapters. It is appropriate, therefore, not to translate the word, but to retain it as a technical term: bamah (plural: bamoth).

iii. bāmâ = '*sanctuary*'

It appears that the word was also used loosely at times to mean not merely one item of the installations at a sacred site, but the entire complex of building that might surround it: to mean something akin to 'shrine/sanctuary'.

Amos vii 9 provides a perfect example of this, for *bāmâ* is made the poetic parallel to 'sanctuary':

> The shrines (*bāmôṯ*) of Isaac shall be desolate;
> The sanctuaries (*miqdᵉšê*) of Israel shall be laid waste.

The same sense is required in 1 Samuel ix 19 where Samuel says to Saul: 'Go before me to the sanctuary (*habbāmâ*), for today you shall eat with me.' Here he is not using the word *bāmâ* simply in the sense of 'platform', but of the whole sanctuary area – for a little later (verse 22) we find Saul eating not on an open-air platform, but in a building. The same sense of 'sanctuary precincts' is required in the three Chronicles references to the *bāmâ* at Gibeon.[38] For instance, 1 Chronicles xvi 39 tells how David left Zadok 'before the tabernacle of Yahweh *in* (or *at*) the sanctuary (*babbāmâ*) that was at Gibeon'.

iv. *The meaning of* bāmôṯ

It has already been noted that there are two forms of the construct plural of *bāmâ* – *bāmᵒṯê* and *bāmôṯ*. The former is only used in one type of context with meanings more or less close to the English word 'flanks'; but it never occurs in any cultic context. This fact prompts the suggestion that at the time that the consonantal text was fixed, these two distinct forms were being used to designate two distinct meanings. In this case *bāmôṯ* will always have a cultic sense – 'bamoth' or 'sanctuaries' – and will never mean 'heights' (the translation chosen in a few passages by RSV and others). An examination of these few doubtful passages shows that there is no reason why the usual cultic sense may not stand in each case.

But before we proceed with this examination, one special feature of the word *bāmôṯ* must be recognised: in our extant texts it can have a singular as well as a plural sense. For there are a number of occurrences of *bāmôṯ* where the context makes it plain that only one structure in one location is being referred to, or that a place-name is being mentioned. In all these cases, *bāmôṯ* will be singular in meaning. These would seem to be 'plurals of local extension'.[39] An alternative explanation may be that in these passages the MT is preserving a variant (but correct) vocalisation of the feminine singular construct, under the influence of Phoenician.[40]

In 2 Kings xxiii 8 there is a very clear instance of a single bamah in one specific location being described by the word *bāmôṯ*:

> And [Josiah] broke down the bamah of the gates (*'eṯ-bāmôṯ haššeʿārîm*)[41] that was at the entrance of the gate of Joshua the governor of the city, which was on one's left at the gate of the city.

Similarly, Jeremiah's various references to *'eṯ-bāmôṯ habbaʿal* or *bāmôṯ hattōp̄eṯ* suggest that only one structure in one location (the Valley of Hinnom) is being referred to.[42]

The same may be true in Micah i 5 (although this is often regarded as being a spurious occurrence of *bāmôṯ*):

> What is the transgression of Jacob?
> Is it not Samaria?
> What is the *bāmôṯ* of Judah?
> Is it not Jerusalem?

bāmôṯ has often been treated as 'a gloss which succeeded in replacing the original text'.[43] One of the reasons for supposing this to have happened is that 'Jerusalem' is not a satisfactory answer to the question 'What are the high places of Judah?'.[44] But if *bāmôṯ* is taken with a singular sense (parallel to singular *pešaʿ* in the previous line), then the Hebrew text may well merit reinstatement.[45] Taken in this sense, Micah is calling Jerusalem the bamah of Judah – referring to the Temple.[46] In this case he will be using 'shocking' language by deliberately employing a word loaded with pagan associations. But to shock his hearers seems to be precisely what this provocative oracle is designed to do.

We are now in a position to examine two passages where *bāmôṯ* has usually been translated 'heights' or 'height', but which should probably be treated as having a singular (and cultic) sense 'bamah' or 'sanctuary'.

Ezekiel xxxvi 2 contains the exultant taunt of Israel's enemy, translated in RSV: 'Aha!' and 'The ancient heights (*ûḇāmôṯ 'ôlām*)[47] have become our possession'. But *bāmôṯ* may quite satisfactorily be given the cultic sense of 'bamah' or 'sanctuary' – referring to the Jerusalem Temple.[48] The taunt will therefore have been: 'The ancient sanctuary has become our possession'[49] – in anticipation of forthcoming acquisitions.

bāmôṯ also occurs in five passages[50] whose context indicates that Moabite place-names are being referred to.[51] Since by its nature a place-name can only refer to one location, the meaning of *bāmôṯ* in these passages will be singular. We may add that it will be cultic, because the word occurs in the simple non-pleonastic form. Thus in Numbers xxi 28 *bāmôṯ 'arnôn* (RSV: 'the heights of Arnon') will be a place whose name means 'bamah (or sanctuary) of/at Arnon'.[52]

v. bāmâ = '*grave-mound*'

It is probable that the word *bāmâ* was also used to describe a grave-mound. This sense, however, was so unusual that it was not understood by the Massoretes, who (in the two most likely cases of its occurrence) pointed the word as בְּמָוֶת.

The first of these passages is the notoriously difficult Isaiah liii 9:

וַיִּתֵּן אֶת־רְשָׁעִים קִבְרוֹ
וְאֶת־עָשִׁיר בְּמֹתָיו

which RSV translates:

> And they made his grave with the wicked
> and with a rich man in his death.

The Dead Sea Scroll (1Q Is[a]) reads the last word as בומתו, which must mean ‘his bamah’ (pointed by Albright as בּוֹמָתוֹ).[53]

Albright has taken this as his key reference in arguing that the cultic bamoth were integrally connected with rites of the dead.[54] But his argument only stands because of a highly speculative (and disputed)[55] emendation of the text. He emends the MT עָשִׁיר (or עשירים read by 1Q Is[a]) to שְׂעִירִים and translates the last line: ‘And his funerary installations with demons’. Leviticus xvii 7 is cited as evidence that ‘demons’ were worshipped (although this passage does not connect such worship with bamoth). So he brings the argument full circle by stating that a bamah was ‘a place of burial where the deceased were interred according to pagan rites, cemetery near an ancient pagan cultic installation’.[56] This is argument in a circle. A totally subjective emendation is made on the basis of an assumed practice; the emended text is then used to demonstrate the existence of the practice!

Albright's emendation is in any case very unsatisfactory. Leviticus xvii 7 does indeed speak of the worship of שְׂעִירִים. But they are not equated or associated with the spirits of dead human beings. Rather they are symbols of fertility. Moreover, not only is the emended line not an obvious parallel to that which precedes it, but the whole context of Isaiah liii 9 is against Albright's interpretation. It is hardly likely that the grave of the dishonoured and ‘wicked’ Servant would be allowed to be near a sanctuary, still less become one.

However, when all this has been said, it is clear that עָשִׁיר can hardly be the original text, since ‘the rich’ is not a satisfactory parallel to ‘the wicked’.[57] עֹשֵׂי רַע is an obvious and long-standing suggested emendation.[58] It is a good parallel both semantically and phonologically to רְשָׁעִים, but is without any textual evidence. But now A. Guillaume[59] has shown that עָשִׁיר may be cognate with the Arabic collective noun غشر meaning ‘the low, base, vile, ignoble, mean or sordid, or the refuse or rabble of mankind’.[60] There may thus be no need to emend the consonantal text at all to have a very forceful parallel to רְשָׁעִים. Whichever emendation be accepted, it is clear that the Servant is being described as being given a dishonouring and perhaps criminal style of burial.

What then are we to make of בּוֹמָתוֹ? In what sense is it parallel to קִבְרוֹ? As we have seen, Albright attempted unsuccessfully to relate them through the cult. I would suggest, however, that the relation is rather to be seen in their *shape*.[61] As we have seen, the primary sense behind *bāmâ* and its cognates was not cultic at all, but was a general one somewhat akin to the English word ‘flank’, which could be used in topographical contexts in some such sense as ‘hillside’. *bāmâ* is thus a very suitable word to describe the large stone cairn – a man-made hill – which commonly was heaped over a dug-grave.

We know from both textual and archaeological evidence that the normal method of burial in Israel was for the corpse to be laid in the family sepulchre. This would either be cut in rock, or be a natural cave.[62] A corpse was not normally inhumed in a grave dug in the soil (as is our Western custom).

However, in emergencies where no sepulchre was available, recourse had to be had to this method. An example is Absalom's corpse which they ‘threw (*wayyašlîḵû*)’ into a large ‘hole (*paḥaṯ*)’ in the ground, and then covered with a large mound of stones (*gal-ʼaḇānîm*).[63] This was probably not only necessary as a wartime emergency measure, but also as a deliberate attempt on the part of Joab to dishonour a traitor. The same seems to have been done in the case of another ‘traitor’, Achan, over whose ashes they raised a large mound of stones (*gal-ʼaḇānîm*).[64] Again, Joshua deliberately put the King of Ai to a dishonourable death by hanging, and then threw (*wayyašlîḵû*) his corpse into a pit,[65] and raised a large mound of stones (*gal-'aḇānîm*) over it. The same form of ignominious death and burial seems to have been reserved for each king whom Joshua defeated.[66]

Similar treatment was given to the corpse of the 'traitor' Uriah, which Jehoiakim 'threw (*wayyašlēḵ*) into the burial place[67] of the common people'.[68] This seems to have been a 'common trench, where the bodies of "stateless persons" and condemned criminals were thrown'.[69] After use, the trench will have been filled in, and presumably a visible mound remained on the spot, as in the above cases. The purpose of these mounds may have been to prevent people defiling themselves by inadvertently walking over a grave.

The *bāmâ* of Isaiah liii 9 will be precisely such a 'mound'. The context makes plain that the Servant is being deliberately dishonoured and treated like a criminal.[70] In the end

> They made his grave with the wicked,
> and his burial-mound with the rabble.

A second passage which Albright cites in support of bamoth being sanctuaries involved with a cult of the dead is Job xxvii 15. This is a passage referring once again to the fate of the 'wicked man (*'āḏām rāšā'*)' (verse 13). His children are killed or starve, while (in the RSV translation):

> Those who survive him the pestilence buries (בַּמָּוֶת יִקָּבֵרוּ),
> and their widows make no lamentation.

Albright notes that once again we have במות and קבר in immediate association, and that the expression 'to be buried in the pestilence' (the literal sense of the MT which the RSV obscures) is of doubtful meaning. He proposes to repoint בַּמָּוֶת as בָּמוֹת, and so without any alteration to the consonantal text, he produces the translation 'His survivors shall be buried in pagan graves'.[71]

I accept this emendation, but not the translation. There is

nothing in the passage to suggest that the burial is related in any way to the cult. Rather the reverse. As in Isaiah liii 9, the stress is on ignominious death. The offspring of the wicked man will not flourish; they will be killed either by war or famine; any that do outlive their father shall be buried in common graves (i.e. they shall not 'sleep with their fathers'), and the customary funeral ceremonies will be omitted. בָּמוֹת will once again refer to the particular type of trench-grave, surmounted by a mound, usually reserved for paupers and criminals. In the context of the whole chapter, the word is clearly loaded with associations, which we may venture to suggest with the translation:

> His survivors shall be buried in paupers' graves,
> and their widows shall not bewail them.

Albright considers that another instance of bamoth in relation to burials occurs in Ezekiel xliii 7. Literally translated, the MT reads:

> The house of Israel shall no more defile my holy name by their harlotry, and by the corpses (*ûḇᵉp̄iḡrê*) of their kings [in] their bamoth (*bāmôṯām*).

Albright, however, translates the last phrase 'by the funerary stelae of their kings in their *bāmôṯ*'.[72]

But once again his theory is only supported by conjectural evidence, which at best is quite inconclusive.[73] No reason is presented for rejecting the long-accepted interpretation of this verse – that *p̄iḡrê* refers quite literally to the corpses of the earlier kings (who, we know, were the only people permitted to be buried actually inside the city). Their presence close to the Temple, together with the presence of paganising prostitution rites within the Temple combine to produce two items which in Ezekiel's mind utterly defile the Temple area. As for *bāmôṯām*, there is good evidence that it should be omitted from the text entirely.[74]

In all, this verse is far too insecure a foundation for the

theory of funerary rites which Albright has built on it. It is probably wisest to dismiss this verse entirely from the discussion of bamoth.

EARLIER FORMS OF 'BĀMÂ'

There remains one last occurrence of *bāmôṯ* which does not satisfactorily fit into any of the above categories – Micah iii 12 = Jeremiah xxvi 18:

> Zion shall be plowed as a field,
> And Jerusalem shall be a heap of ruins,
> And the mountain of the House (*lᵉḇāmôṯ yāʿar*).

How to translate the last phrase has been a problem since the days of the LXX.[75] The plural *bāmôṯ* is impossible to reconcile with the single site referred to. The problem remains whichever of the common meanings of *bāmâ* is selected. But even if it is taken in the singular sense 'sanctuary/bamah' it does not satisfactorily link with the following word *yāʿar*.

The common translation[76] 'wooded height' is unsatisfactory on many counts: it ignores the plural; it overlooks the fact that the meaning 'heights' is only connected with the pleonastic form *bāmᵒṯê* (which Micah both knows and uses – i 3); it suggests a symbol of plenty instead of a symbol of desolation, which the context certainly demands; the translation of *yāʿar* by 'wooded' is probably illegitimate, as the idiom is found nowhere else.

However if לְבָמוֹת be understood as a contracted form of לְבַהֲמוֹת,[77] we have an excellent parallel:

> Zion shall be ploughed as a field,
> And Jerusalem shall be a heap of ruins,
> And the mountain of the House (shall belong)
> to the beasts of the forest.

D. R. Hillers[78] has shown how perfectly this fits into the commonest of curse themes – that a city will become the dwelling place of wild animals. The exact phrase *bah^a môṯ ya'ar* occurs elsewhere in Micah's own book (v 7), while the parallel phrase *ḥay^e ṯô-yā'ar* is found in Psalms l 10 (as a parallel to *b^e hēmôṯ*) and civ 20. Hillers suggests that the spelling in the MT is not a transcriptional error, but phonetic spelling of the word as it was actually pronounced.

Another case where *b^e hēmâ* seems to occur in a contracted form is Isaiah ii 22,[79] which RSV translates:

> Turn away from man
> in whose nostrils is breath,
> for of what account is he?
> (כי בַמֶּה נחשב הוא)

But this is forced. There is no other instance of the construction חשב בְּ'.[80] However, if בַמֶּה be pointed בָּמָה,[81] we get the excellent contrasting parallel:

> Turn away from man,
> in whose nostrils is divine breath[82]
> but who must be considered a beast.[83]

Both these passages seem to indicate that *b^e hēmâ* and *bāmâ* may at one time have been both pronounced and written alike. This has prompted the suggestion[84] that the two words may be etymologically related: that *b^e hēmâ* may preserve an earlier form of *bāmâ*. This may well be so, as the following semantic and morphological pointers seem to indicate. But with the scant evidence available, certainly is not to be expected.

Like *bāmâ*, *b^e hēmâ* has no known verbal root in Hebrew.[85] In extant texts it means 'animal/beast', either domestic or wild. When used of wild animals, it is not used of wild-life in general, but of mammals, as distinct from birds, reptiles and fish.[86] It is an attractive idea that this could be a specialised meaning derived from the primary meaning 'rib-cage, body, flank', the sequence of semantic development being: flank > flank of an animal > animal. (It will be observed that the type of creature described by *b^e^hēmâ* does in fact have a large 'flank'.)

If it be accepted that *bāmâ* and *b^e^hēmâ* are different derivations from the same root word, the question arises whether *b^e^hēmâ* may preserve the original consonantal form of *bāmâ*. Albright considers that it does.

He suggests than an earlier form (or possible a dialectic variant) of *bāmâ* was *bômâ*, and that this form is preserved in 1Q Is^a^. He notes that 'in the same Qumrân MS we now find six certain occurrences of the word . . . in three cases we find the spelling *bômāh* and in three others the spelling *bâmāh* (without *waw*)'.[87] Elsewhere he compares *bômâ* with the Greek βωμός meaning 'raised platform'. Βωμός is generally accepted as being of non-Greek origin.[88] It is possible therefore that the Greeks borrowed the word from the Phoenicians, and preserved the old form *bômâ*, current at the time the borrowing was made.[89]

Albright considers that all this indicates that 'the original form of the word was almost certainly **bahmatu*'.[90] Subsequently, this was variously pronounced as *bōhmah* and *bāhmah*; the medial *h* then quiesced, leaving the two forms *bômâ* and *bāmâ*. He finds a parallel to such a development in the word *qôl* 'voice', which derives not from **qawlu/qaulu*, but from **qahlu* 'call', which in turn is from the root *qhl* 'to call, assemble'.

While Albright may well be right in asserting **bahmatu* to be the original form of *bāmâ*, we should note that this is only conjecture, and falls short of proof. It could be an equally justifiable conjecture to suggest that *bômâ* and *bāmâ* both derive from **bûm*, and to cite the parallel *qômâ* 'height' and *qāmâ* 'standing grain' which both derive from *qûm* 'to arise'. However, this conjecture would involve denying that *b^e^hēmâ* has any etymological relationship to *bāmâ*, whereas the close semantic link between the two words suggests the contrary.

SEMANTIC DEVELOPMENT

There are thus strong indications of an etymological link between the two Hebrew variants *bāmâ* and *bômâ* on the one hand with the Greek βωμός, and on the other with the Akkadian *bamtu* and *bamâtu* and the Ugaritic *bmt*; it is also possible that the word *b^e^hēmâ* may preserve an older form behind all six words. Is there any *semantic* link between these six words (or seven if *b^e^hēmâ* be included) with their various meanings – including *bāmâ* with its most common cultic meaning?

We may begin by noting that the primary sense behind all the words under discussion (excepting the Hebrew cultic sense) is ‘rib-cage’. But many derived meanings are evident in a variety of contexts. An ‘umbrella’ meaning in English which covers most or these contexts is ‘flank’ (if one thinks of the flank as being the rib area).

Thus in both Akkadian and Ugaritic the word can mean ‘chest’ (‘flank’ of a man) or ‘thorax’ (‘flank’ of riding animal or slaughtered ox). A virtually identical anatomical sense in Hebrew occurs in Deuteronomy xxxiii 29 and Job ix 8, although in the context of ‘treading upon the “flanks” (*bām^o^ṯê*) of enemies/sea-monster’ the translation ‘back(s)’ is more suitable in English.

In the form *b^e^hēmâ*, the sense may have developed further – to mean not any single part of an animal, but the creature itself. It is significant that this word is used especially of sheep and cattle – animals distinguished by the size of their ‘flanks’ and used for meat.

But in at least two languages, the word was applied not only to animate creatures, but also topographically. Thus in Akkadian one could speak of the ‘flanks of the mountains’ (? and in Ugaritic of ‘flanks of the earth’): in other words ‘hill-sides’. This seems to be precisely the sense required of *bāmôṯeḵā* in 2 Samuel i 19 and 25 against the background of Jonathan’s being killed on the slopes of Gilboa.

But apart from this one 'secular' instance of the topographical use of *bāmᵒṯê*, it is only found in a very special context – a mythological one where Yahweh is described as 'treading on the flanks of the earth' (i.e. 'mountains'). Nevertheless, the concept of 'flank' is still associated with the word in this mythological phrase, for on two occasions[91] the accompanying verb is 'to mount upon (*rkb 'l*)'. Since *rkb 'l* is the common way of speaking of mounting upon a camel, horse, mule, etc., we must suppose that the mountains are visualised as being steeds for a rider. To describe them as 'flanks of the earth' is thus particularly apt in view of the Akkadian and Ugaritic use of the word for riding animals.

A further extension of this topographical sense is evident in the two cases where Hebrew *bāmâ* means 'grave-mound' – i.e. artificial hill-slopes heaped over a burial.

There remains *bāmâ* in its cultic sense. As we shall see below, the word in a cultic context usually refers to constructed stone platforms used for cultic rites. To date, it has been common to suppose that these structures were called *bāmôṯ* because they were raised up (i.e. were 'heights') above the surrounding ground level. Thus Albright dogmatically states,[92] 'There was only one certain fact . . . which was that the word *bâmāh* had the original meaning (at least in Hebrew) of "height, hill, mound".'

By contrast, de Vaux is rightly more cautious in his definition: 'The idea which the word expresses . . . is something which stands out in relief from its background, but the idea of a mountain or hill is not contained in the word itself.'[93] For, as we have noted above, the idea of height is not present in *bāmâ*, and so cannot be the semantic link between the cultic sense of Hebrew *bāmâ* and the other senses. There seems to be a caesura at this point which can perhaps only be explained by supposing that the cultic sense was *coined* (? in Israel) in the context of a particular cult mythology.

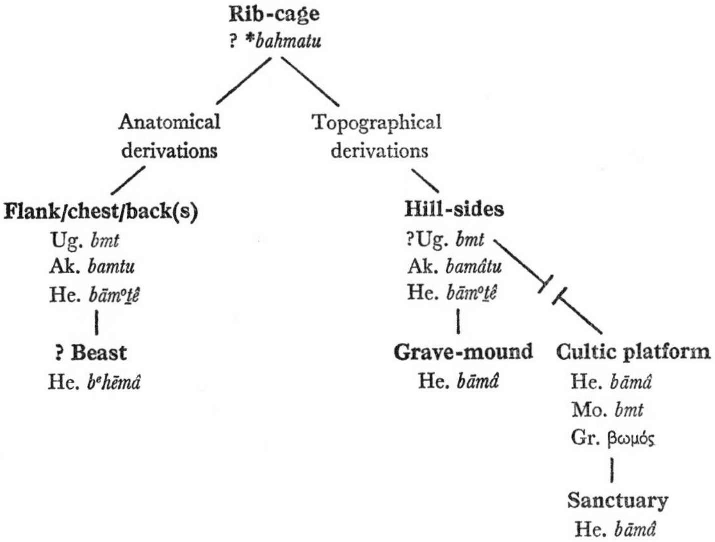

Thus the clue to the problem will lie in the cultic purpose to which these platforms were put, and the mythology with which they were connected.

We know from the passages already quoted that there was a Hebrew myth about Yahweh appearing in theophany, in the course of which he is described in archaic ritual language as 'treading on the *bām^{o}ṯê* of the land'. Closely associated with this myth is the belief that Yahweh in time of danger would come victoriously to the rescue of his protégé, and cause him to share his position upon *bām^{o}ṯê* of the land.

The suggestion here made is that bamoth were originally constructed in order to actualise this mythology in a cultic ritual. What more natural than that these man-made structures should be designated by the names of the objects they represented? These structures continued in use until the Exile, by which time they were known simply as bamoth.

A further extension of the cultic sense of *bāmâ* developed as the word came to be applied not only to the cultic platform, but to the whole site surrounding it – the 'sanctuary'.

As the Greeks encountered these cultic platforms, they will have adopted the appropriate Semitic word to describe them. Thus βωμός entered the Greek language as a cultic word: 'altar' remains its commonest sense. So Hebrew, which is all but unique among Semitic languages in making the cultic sense of *bāmâ* its common one, is not alone.

The above discussion may be summarised in the diagram of semantic (but not etymological) development on p. 25.

ALBRIGHT'S FURTHER OBSERVATIONS

Before going on to discuss the Biblical and archaeological evidence regarding the nature of cultic bamoth, some further etymological observations of Albright need examination.

He holds the view[94] that bamoth were in the first place burial cairns or artificial mounds of stone, and sometimes not a mound at all, but an upright stele set up in honour of some worthy. These sites were later regarded as suitable for cultic shrines. He attempts to find etymological support for this contention.

He notes that the Akkadian *ubān* meant 'summit (of the mountains)', whereas the closely related word *ubānu* meant 'a finger'. Assuming that the original form of *bāmâ* was *bahmat*, he proceeds to compare this Akkadian word with the Hebrew for 'thumb', *bôhen*, and also with the Arabic *'ibhām* (meaning the same), both of which he claims retain the medial *h*. He sees the word *bôhen* as preserving yet another meaning of *bāmâ*: 'an upright, finger-like, post or stele'.

Albright further observes that medieval Arabic lexicographers noted[95] the obscure and otherwise unknown word *buhmatun* as meaning 'a mass of rock', with the secondary meaning 'hero, brave man'. What is the connection between these two meanings? Albright mistakenly sees it in rock high places, and cites the example of the (so called) Conway High Place at Petra, a mass of natural rock with associated structures built around it, which he takes to be a funerary high place.

So he sums up his evidence by asserting that 'the etymological picture is now sufficiently clear to enable us to set up a basic meaning "projecting mass of rock, mountain ridge, stone burial cairn" for Heb. *bâmāh*, "high place" '.[96] This last assertion is dubious in the extreme, being built up on sheer speculation. His reasoning is based on two points, neither of which survives scrutiny.

First there is the etymological argument. Here Albright's logic is at fault. He wishes to prove the existence of an Israelite hero-cult based around rocks. To do this he draws on an obscure Arabic word. This word has two meanings which can only be connected together by assuming an Arab custom parallel to the assumed Israelite custom of a hero-cult based round a rock. This is argument in a circle and proves nothing.

Moreover, Albright's deductions from the meaning of the Arabic *buhmatun* are extremely suspect. So far from referring to dead heroes who were venerated at rock shrines (as he would have us believe), the word was used of men who were very much alive. The subsequent entries by Lane make it clear that, as most generally used, *buhmatun* referred to a man (or men or army) who so confused and daunted his opponents that they knew not how to attack; or it could refer to a 'difficult affair . . . such that one cannot find a way to perform it or manage it'. It would appear to be closely related to the verb meaning 'it (a thing or affair) was or became dubious, confused, or vague so that one knew not the way it should be engaged in'.[97]

As regards the meaning 'mass of rock' attached to *buhmatun*, the full meaning as given by Tāj el-'Arūs (which Albright does not quote completely) clarifies its connection with the above: 'a rock or great mass of stone or of hard rock that is solid, not hollow' – the implication being that its daunting character makes it difficult to know how it should be split or quarried,[98] or in some way used. The word may thus be understood without any resort to the cultus.

Secondly, there is the archaeological argument. Albright's assumption that the Israelites had a hero-cult which centred round a mass of rock springs largely from his conviction that he had found such a rock in the (so called) Conway High Place. He claims that 'the earliest bamah-high place was very much like the Conway High Place'.[99] But, as we shall see in Chapter III, the Conway High Place cannot now be regarded as a High Place at all. Albright has made a false 'identification'.

This being so, his attempt to find a semantic link between the Hebrew *bāmâ* and the Arabic *buhmatun* – meaning (i) mass of rock, (ii) hero – suffers a fatal blow. For he uses the Conway 'High Place' (and the supposed hero-cult behind it) as the clue to the connection between meanings (i) and (ii). However, if the Conway 'High Place' has no cultic significance at all, then there is no reason to suppose that the connection between the two meanings is to be seen *in the cult*. As already shown, study of the Arabic usage of the word has led independently to the same conclusion.

Thus *buhmatun* can teach us nothing about the meaning of *bāmâ*. This has important bearing on the validity of Albright's theory that *bāmâ* could also mean 'an upright, finger-like, post or stele'.

There exists no Hebrew text which may conclusively be shown to require *bāmâ* to be understood in this way.[100] However, there does exist a well-used Hebrew technical term which connotes just such an object — *maṣṣēḇâ*. There is thus a *prima facie* case against *bāmâ* meaning the same thing.[101]

The philology which Albright adduces in support of his contention is scattered, and its sometimes questionable relation to *bāmâ*[102] is found only through his supposed link between *buhmatun* and *bāmâ*. However, now that this link has been shown to be illusory, *bāmâ*'s supposed meaning of 'stele' falls away. Hence Albright's attempt to see a hero-cult as bound into the etymology of *bāmâ* has no foundation whatever.

CHAPTER II

THE OLD TESTAMENT EVIDENCE ON THE NATURE OF BAMOTH

The aim of this chapter is to examine the contexts within which the Old Testament mentions bamoth. On the whole, this evidence is only of a very general, non-specific kind – which no doubt explains why for centuries Biblical scholars have been perplexed as to what a bamah was. But the text occasionally contains confirmatory evidence that bamoth were platforms on which certain cultic rites were performed.

THE LOCATION AND CONSTRUCTION OF BAMOTH

Most usually bamoth were situated on high ground. Thus Samuel 'goes up' to, and 'comes down from' an unnamed bamah.[1] Saul meets prophets 'coming down from' the bamah at Gibeath-elohim.[2] Solomon builds pagan bamoth 'on the mountain east of Jerusalem'.[3] The bamah at Bethel appears also to have been situated on a mountain.[4] These four references are from widely differing periods, and all four bamoth were on high ground. They are not isolated cases, for the traditional Deuteronomic description of bamoth is 'on every high hill, and under every green tree',[5] thus indicating that high ground was the most common location of bamoth.

However, not all bamoth were on hills in the open country with trees growing on them. Some were to be found within city walls, or even in low-lying valleys.

There are several references in the Book of Kings[6] which seem to suggest that there were bamoth actually *inside* the cities of Samaria and Judah. A typical statement is 2 Kings xvii 9:

> They built for themselves bamoth in all their towns, from watch-tower to fortified city.

Jerusalem itself was no exception: there seems to have been a bamah actually beside the gate of Joshua[7] 'on the left as one enters[8] the city gate'.

There are also several references outside the Book of Kings which indicate the presence of bamoth inside cities. Ezekiel xvi 15–25 is the most detailed account in the whole Bible of what happened at a city bamah. In his parable of the foundling, the prophet describes how 'she made . . . gaily decked bamoth' on which she played the harlot (verse 16). Subsequently he mentions (verses 23–5) where these bamoth were situated, and indicates that they were specially built structures within a city:

> You built yourself a mound (*gāḇ*) and made yourself a lofty place (*rāmâ*) in every square, at the head of every street you built your lofty place and prostituted your beauty.

The *gāḇ* and *rāmâ* will be words describing the appearance of a city bamah.[9]

But bamoth could also be found on low-lying ground, as Ezekiel vi 3 suggests:

> Thus says the Lord GOD to the mountains and the hills, to the ravines and the valleys . . . I will destroy your bamoth.

One particular bamah is specifically stated to have been built in a valley: 'They built *'eṯ-bāmôṯ habba'al* in the valley of the sons of Hinnom.'[10] Clearly the traditional translation 'high place' is inappropriate to what is in fact a geographical depression; *bāmôṯ* in this passage will most certainly refer to an artificially built platform sited in a valley.

Such an interpretation of bamoth is borne out by all the Biblical references to their construction or destruction. It is clear that they were man-made. They are commonly spoken of as being 'built' (√*bnh*). When they are removed, they are 'torn down' (√*nts̩*),[11] a word always used of stone-built structures such as altars, walls, houses; or 'destroyed' (√*'bd*);[12] or simply 'removed' (√*swr*).[13]

Such is the evidence on the nature of a bamah which we may cull from the contexts of the actual occurrences of the word *bāmâ* in the Old Testament.

THE RITES AT OR ON BAMOTH

Since the Old Testament (especially in the Deuteronomic writings) was more concerned to decry than to describe bamoth, the evidence for the cult associated with them is all too slight. Six activities may however be traced: the burning of incense,[14] sacrificing, the eating of attendant sacrificed meals,[15] praying,[16] prostitution,[17] and child sacrifice.[18]

Two of these rites we may definitely say were performed *upon* the bamah. Isaiah depicts Moab wearying 'himself upon the bamah (*'al-habbāmâ*) when he comes to his sanctuary to pray'.[16] While Ezekiel upbraids the people because they made 'gaily decked bamoth and on them (*'ᵃlêhem*) played the harlot'.[17]

Of the precise location of the other rites we cannot be so certain. The typical Deuteronomic phrase is that 'the people still sacrificed and burned incense *babbāmôṯ*'.[19] Unfortunately this oft-recurring phrase is ambiguous, and may mean either *upon* the bamoth (platforms), or *at* the bamoth (sanctuaries). In view of the archaeological evidence to be discussed in the next chapter, the former sense cannot be ruled out.

If, for the moment, it be granted that sacrifices were made directly on the bamah, then clearly the bamah was being used as an altar. We might, therefore, reasonably expect to find some indication in the Biblical texts that bamoth were regarded as altars. That this is in fact the case seems to be supported by the manner in which cultic furniture is listed.

In the Books of Kings there are many passages listing pagan cult items either set up by kings who 'did what was evil in the eyes of the LORD', or removed by kings who 'did what was right'. In these lists, bamoth are grouped with *maṣṣēḇôṯ*, *'ašērîm*, and images, etc.[20] But, despite the frequent references the Books of Kings make to sacrifices at bamoth,[19] *mizbeḥôṯ* are never included in these lists.[21] Mention of bamoth seems to preclude mention of altars. This suggests that the words were synonymous (at least to the Deuteronomic writers).

This is in fact how these two words seem to have been used on at least two occasions in the Books of Kings, and failure to recognise them as synonymous has made one of the passages notoriously difficult to interpret. It is 2 Kings xxiii 15, which in RSV reads:

> Moreover the altar at Bethel, the high place erected by Jeroboam the son of Nebat, who made Israel to sin, that altar with the high place he [Josiah] pulled down and broke in pieces its stones [Gk: Heb 'he burned the high place'], crushing them to dust; also he burned the Asherah.

The MT of this verse is usually regarded as being untranslatable, and interpolations are assumed to be present.[22] *BH*³, for instance, suggests that probably all three occurrences of *habbāmâ* should be excised as additions or corruptions. This is unnecessary however if the bamah be thought of as the altar itself (or possibly the platform on which the altar stood).

The curious phrase 'The altar which is at Bethel the bamah' may be allowed to stand – the bamah being identified with the altar, and grammatically in apposition to it. After the parenthesis about Jeroboam, the same phrase is again taken up: 'that altar, the bamah,[23] he pulled down[24] and broke in pieces its stones,[25] grinding them to dust; and he burned the Asherah'. The confusion in the present MT will have arisen because *habbāmâ* was thought of as meaning 'sanctuary'. The first occurrence of the word was left untouched, because grammatically it could be thought of as in apposition to 'Bethel'. On the second occurrence it had to be distinguished from 'that altar' by the insertion of 'and', thus suggesting that both the altar *and* the sanctuary surrounding it were pulled down. Precisely what happened over the third occurrence of the word is now impossible to determine, as it is bound up with the corruption of the adjacent verb, where an original *wyšbr* (cf. LXX) became confused with the neighbouring verb *wyśrp*.

The second passage where *bāmâ* seems to be synonymous with *mizbēaḥ* is 1 Kings iii 4:

> The king went to Gibeon to sacrifice there, for that was the great high place (*habbāmâ haggᵉḏôlâ*); Solomon used to offer a thousand burnt offerings upon that altar (*ham-mizbēaḥ hahû'*).

The expression 'that altar' seems to suppose a previous mention of the altar, which is not (overtly) the case. However, if *habbāmâ haggᵉḏôlâ* be seen as meaning 'the chief (altar-)platform'[26] rather than 'the chief sanctuary', then this difficulty disappears.

We may thus conclude that the Biblical text[27] contains a number of indications which suggest (a) that sometimes (possibly normally) sacrifices were offered directly upon a bamah, and (b) that as a result of this practice, *bāmâ* was sometimes used as a synonym for *mizbēaḥ*. Archaeological evidence (which we shall examine in the next chapter) confirms (a), and certain LXX translations support (b).

THE LXX TRANSLATIONS OF 'BĀMÂ'

The LXX translates *bāmâ* in over a dozen different ways. The most frequently used Greek translation is τὸ ὑψηλόν[28] (over fifty times). However, on at least seven occasions[29] βωμός is used. We have already noted how Albright drew attention to the close philological relation between βωμός and *bāmâ*. What he does not fully draw attention to, however, is the meaning that the Greeks attached to the word, and the fact that the word itself is actually used in the LXX to translate *bāmâ*.

LSJ[30] give eight known meanings of βωμός. 'Raised platform' is witnessed by only three references: twice in Homer of a stand for chariots, and a base for a statue,[31] and once elsewhere of the base for a sarcophagus.[32] This meaning is noted by Albright, but he fails to stress the fact that the word is only used of a platform *on which to stand something*, and is thus not the kind of platform produced by a cairn of stones piled over a grave.[33]

From the time of Homer onwards, βωμός was the word commonly used to designate the object upon which one offered sacrifice.[34] However, we should notice that βωμός could describe not only the actual altar itself, but also the cultic platform on which the altar stood, or which perhaps even took the place of the altar. Thus there are many references to suppliants sitting actually *on* the βωμός.[35] Such a βωμός will have been a low flat platform, large enough to accommodate several people. In such a context, the word βωμός is being used with a sense very close to its primary (secular) meaning of 'raised platform, base'.

In other words, the basic concept behind βωμός is not cultic at all, but is of any object of a particular shape (oblong) which had a particular function (serving as base or plinth to something). This is borne out by two derivatives of βωμός. *LSJ* list fourteen compounds and derivations, all but two of which are connected with the altar idea. The two exceptions are significant because they illustrate the wider concept behind βωμός.

One, βωμίς, a diminutive of βωμός, is used by Herodotus[36] to describe the step formation of the pyramids. The other, βωμόσπειρα has a similar meaning: 'the round base of a column *placed on a square plinth*'.[37] Neither of these two words can be connected with βωμός through the cult. The connection will be geometric: common to all three words is the concept of an oblong structure which, according to its function, could be described as a 'step, plinth, base, platform'.

It is thus all the more interesting to find that on at least seven occasions βωμός was the word chosen to represent *bāmâ*. Probably the phonological similarity between the two words made βωμός an attractive choice. But in view of the common meaning 'altar, altar–platform' attached to the Greek word, we are bound to suppose that the LXX translators understood that this common meaning of βωμός adequately conveyed to a Greek-speaker what a bamah was: a cultic platform or altar.

This conclusion is confirmed by the fact that they actually used βωμός to translate *mizbēaḥ* twenty times.[38] In each case it is pagan altars that are being referred to – never the recognised altars of Yahweh.[39] Θυσιαστήριον is invariably the word used to translate the latter in the LXX of the books within the Hebrew Canon. 1 Maccabees also preserves the same distinction.[40] However, in the later Jewish writings (e.g. ben Sira, 2 Maccabees, Josephus), this restricted understanding of βωμός is not found: they use βωμός interchangeably with θυσιαστήριον when speaking of the altar of the Lord in the Temple.[41]

This contrast between the early and later Graeco-Jewish use of βωμός only serves to heighten the restricted meaning of the word when used in the LXX prophetic books to represent *bāmâ*. Clearly in these passages the translators understood bamoth to be pagan altars.

This LXX understanding of *bāmâ* thus provides additional grounds for supposing that sacrifices were offered directly on a bamah, and that *bāmâ* was regarded as a synonym for *mizbēaḥ*.

THE GEOGRAPHICAL DISTRIBUTION OF BAMOTH

It was noted earlier that while several Semitic languages have some form of the word *bāmâ*, it is only in Hebrew literature that the word is to be found with a cultic sense. The single exception to this statement is the occurrence of the word *bmt* in line 3 of the Mesha Inscription: ואעש הבמת זאת לכמש – 'and I made this *bmt* for Kemosh'. The *bmt* is obviously cultic, and is thus clear evidence that the Moabites also had bamoth as a necessary part of their cult.

In view of this, it is all the more significant that the Old Testament contains no fewer than nine references to bamoth in relation to Moab: five times of Moabite place-names which incorporate the word *bāmôṯ*,[42] and four times in direct mentions of the Moabite cult, either as practised in Moab itself,[43] or as an imported religion in Judah.[44]

The Ammonites appear also to have used bamoth, since Solomon had to build a bamah in order to worship Molech.[44] But as to what extent other nations used bamoth we must remain agnostic. Certainly outside the Canaanite(Hebrew)–Ammonite–Moabite region there is neither literary nor archaeological evidence of their existence.

CHAPTER III

ARCHAEOLOGICAL EVIDENCE ON THE NATURE OF BAMOTH

Because a bamah was a solid structure made in durable material, it is only to be expected that some examples may have been preserved down into our time. True, the traditional Deuteronomic description suggests that rural bamoth were of such a rudimentary nature that nothing would have survived of them. But in richer centres we might expect that traces would be left of their more elaborate structures. Despite the hazards surrounding the 'identification' of cultic sites,[1] we may safely say that excavation has laid bare actual examples of bamoth.

However, we may note here that some excavators have used the word 'bamah' too freely in their descriptions of their finds. For example, natural rock outcrops with artificial hollows cut in them have sometimes been described as 'bamoth' or (in translation) 'high places'.[2] While such natural altars undoubtedly existed, we are not justified in describing them by the word 'bamoth', which in our extant texts always describes a man-made structure. Apart from one classic misidentification, such rock-altars will not therefore be discussed in what follows.

A MISIDENTIFICATION

At the outset, one would-be claimant to the title 'bamah' must be dismissed: the so-called 'Conway High Place' at Petra. It was discovered by Agnes Conway in 1929, who in her report[3] described it as 'a natural rock altar, enclosed by a wall because it was sacred'. She later excavated it with the help of Albright,[4] who assigned the task of writing the definitive report to R. L. Cleveland.[5] Convinced beforehand that they were excavating a cultic site, everything found was 'interpreted' in a cultic sense. The fact that by 1960 Albright (in *HPAP*) had 'convincingly explained the word *bâmāh* as a development of an older form **bahmatu*, which had the basic meaning "projecting mass of rock"'[6] only confirmed Cleveland in his 'interpretation'.

And all this despite the glaring fact that there is not a single piece of evidence in the Old Testament for the existence of such bamoth. Bamoth are always spoken of as being 'built', whilst when destroyed they are spoken of as being 'torn down'. Both these expressions are inappropriate with regard to a mass of natural rock. Neither are there any references in the Old Testament to processions around sacred rocks (rites which Cleveland assumes took place at the 'Conway High Place'). The little evidence that he does adduce in support of the practice of processing around a rock is from the late Arab period, and he fails to demonstrate that it has any bearing whatever on cultic practices in the Old Testament period.[7]

However, the ghost of the 'Conway High Place' has now been finally laid by P. J. Parr, who has undertaken a further examination of the site.[8] He has shown that 'it has absolutely nothing to do with Nabatean cult practices, but represents a purely military structure, a round tower at the corner of Petra's ramparts'.[9] Although the details of his work need not be repeated here, a summary of the points which touch on Albright's and Cleveland's cultic interpretation is in place, because their full significance for Old Testament studies has not yet been stressed.

Parr has decisively shown that this tower was part of Petra's defence system in that he has discovered traces of the two walls which abutted on to either side of the tower.[10] This site was included within the city area because it is a natural eminence with an excellent view of approaches to Petra. The natural outcrop of rock was an ideal site for a corner tower (there is a steep escarpment on one side of it), and its foundations were able to be set in a trench cut into the rock. What Albright took to be the rock-cut stairway (of the 'processional way' around the 'sacred rock') is in fact this foundation trench. Parr found traces of the wall foundations in the trench, but most of its remains had been systematically removed by the earlier excavators mistakenly thinking it was debris filling the 'staircase'.[11]

There were however two matters of obvious cultic significance which strengthened Albright in his cultic interpretation of the whole site:[12] the discovery of a small stone altar and pedestal to the side of the tower, and the presence of a number of pots buried upright in the 'debris' of the trench. Against this Parr says 'There is no necessary connection between their [the altar and pedestal's] undoubted religious character and the nature of the original monument. The presence of a later sanctuary cannot serve in favour of Albright's hypothesis touching the circular monument itself'.[13] As for the pots: 'The greater part of the material is later in date than the abandonment of the tower.'[14] They belong to the second to third centuries A.D., at which time the city walls had contracted, leaving the site outside Petra. It was then used as a cemetery. 'Identical pots buried in a vertical position and sometimes associated with the burials of children have been found in a Nabatean building recently excavated in Petra, where they seem to date from the 2nd century of our era *after* the destruction of the building.'[15]

So let the 'Conway High Place' change its name to the Conway Round Tower. Cleveland's statement that 'the earliest *bâmāh*-high places were very much like the Conway High Place', whose 'discovery and excavation have contributed significantly to our knowledge of the ancient Semitic high place'[16] could hardly be further from the truth.

TYPE I BAMOTH

Several structures regarded by their excavators as bamoth have been found. In the descriptions of them which follow there is nothing new; but they are here repeated (using as far as possible the excavators' own words) because in certain details they illustrate very clearly the physical characteristics of a bamah.

Nahariya

The first and most certainly identified bamah was excavated by M. Dothan at Nahariya.[17] It formed the focal point of a complex of cultic structures built 'on a low hillock rising some 2 m above its surroundings'[18] – not a great height, but nevertheless a prominent spot (considering the surrounding flat coastal plain), and just outside the local settlement.[19] During all three phases of development of the site (seventeenth to early sixteenth century B.C.) the bamah was the focus of interest.

At the first stage it abutted on to the south wall of a small shrine building (6 m × 6 m), and consisted of 'a conglomeration of stones (rubble and pebbles) laid directly on the *kurkur* [virgin soil]. This *bamah* was probably roughly circular, with a diameter of about 6 m. The wealth of objects found on the stones of this *bamah* and in its immediate vicinity bear witness to its character as a high place.'[20] These objects were 'animal bones mixed with ashes, pottery and other objects'.

In the second stage a larger temple was built further away, and 'the small *bamah* was enlarged and extended . . . forming a circle with a diameter of about 14 m[21] . . . a flight of two steps made of large flat stones was laid, leading up to the centre of the *bamah*. Between the closely packed stones of the ring-shaped *bamah* and on them we found a dark oily matter which had hardened in the course of time.'[20] In the final stage, the floor of the surrounding courtyard rose covering part of the ancient bamah. But it remained the focus, for a small structure was erected on the centre of the bamah to emphasise it.

Megiddo

Dothan himself compares this bamah to that at Megiddo, to which we now turn. We may let the excavator, G. Loud, describe it. 'At the *highest point*[22] of Stratum XVII lie the lowest courses of a rounded structure (4017) which we unhesitatingly term an altar. For, while evidently destroyed to this level and later rebuilt in similar shape . . . it continues to occupy this exact site through Stratum XIV, a persistence characteristic of sacred structures or areas; its surrounding debris was filled with pot fragments and animal bones . . . surely indicative of sacrifice; and in every stratum it is set apart by an inclosure wall . . . It is roughly elliptical in shape with its major axis of some 10 metres . . . Its minor axis is approximately 8.70 m.[23]

'In Stratum XVI altar 4017 was built to its full height . . . the new structure rises to a minimum height of 1.40 m. Its original summit was reached by a flight of steps at the east . . . Its shape, while approximately that of the base, is now more circular, about 8 meters in diameter at the present top. Its sides taper in varying degree. The entire structure, which is still standing, is of stone, solid so far as the broken west face could show.'[24] (See plates 1(a) and 1(b).)

En-Gedi

A further example of a bamah in a sacred enclosure may have been found in 1962 near En-Gedi – though this example illustrates sharply the difficulty of ascribing to a structure the name 'bamah'. The preliminary excavation report described how 'on top of a mountain which overshadows the spring of En-Gedi, the excavators laid bare a sacred enclosure from the chalcolithic period . . . The enclosure . . . comprises a large courtyard surrounded by two buildings and a gatehouse. In the middle of the courtyard was a little round structure, perhaps a "high place". The principal building . . . was certainly used for cult purposes.'[25] This conclusion was supported by finds in it of a figurine and other cult objects.

However, recent discussion is more guarded in the terminology used to describe the round structure: 'a circular installation, ten feet in diameter, built in the highest part of the courtyard . . . In its centre a round basin, about sixteen inches deep and a foot in diameter, was constructed. At present seven large flat stones form the wall of the basin, the bottom being the natural surface; but assuming that the basin was meant to contain liquids, it must have been plastered.'[26] It seems probable that the En-Gedi Temple was the centre of a 'water cult' – the more likely on account of its proximity to the springs of En-Gedi.

Is this circular installation a bamah, specially adapted for a water cult? Any dogmatic conclusion is out of place. But similarities with the bamoth of Nahariya and Megiddo are obvious: a low circular structure with a flat top, built of rough stones on high ground, in the centre of a cultic enclosure.

Tell Arad

Recent excavations at Tell Arad (1962–7) have revealed several sanctuaries from Israelite times on the same spot. The earliest (Stratum XII, eleventh century B.C.) was a simple affair, reminiscent of that at En-Gedi. The excavator, Y. Aharoni, claims to have found a bamah there: 'This high-place adorned the summit of the hill and was surrounded by the open village occupying the lower slopes. It consisted of a paved area some 100 feet long, enclosed by a temenos wall about three feet thick. On the northern side of the pavement, remnants of a square, stone-built altar was found. South of it was a crescent-shaped *bamah* filled with bricks. Near the altar, we encountered many pits with burnt bones and the burnt skeleton of a young lamb, lacking the head. The fragment of a well-smoothed basalt slab found near it is probably a broken *massebah*.'[27] On the evidence presented, we must be cautious in accepting Aharoni's ready identification of the crescent-shaped object filled with bricks as a bamah, since no bamah of this shape has ever yet been found.[28]

As the settlement grew into a city, the top of the hill was surrounded by a strong citadel wall. The ancient sanctuary was thus included within the citadel, and gave place to a more elaborate temple on the same site – thus illustrating once again the permanent sacred value attached to sites once marked by an ancient bamah. A most striking material illustration of this concept is supplied by a unique 'stone seal with a peculiar design, apparently a representation of the general layout of the fortress'.[29] On this seal 'the temple is depicted as a high, rounded structure'. Aharoni is uncertain how to interpret this – 'Had the temple really a rounded roof, or is this only an artistic impression of its outstanding importance?' I suggest that this may in fact be an accurate representation of a conical bamah, set in a walled enclosure.[30] The curious thing is that in Stratum IX (where the seal was found) the sanctuary should be represented by a type of bamah which was displaced by an elaborate temple well over a century earlier. The seal may, of course, have already been an antique. On the other hand, it is possible that in the mind of the seal-maker his modern elaborate temple only achieved significance because of the known tradition of an ancient bamah on the same site. He thus symbolically represented his temple – by a bamah.

Tumuli near Jerusalem

A whole group of bamoth actually dating from the late monarchy period are located in a series of about twenty tumuli on mountain ridges near Jerusalem.[31] 'Most characteristic and common to all is the shape – a truncated cone with a small flat area on the top and steep slopes.'[32] They 'have changed the natural outlines of the landscape'[33] – a description reminiscent of the other meanings of *bāmâ* – for although scattered over an area of several square miles, all the sites are 'on ridges well above their surroundings and overlook far distances'.[32] Several of these have been excavated.

One (no. 5) had as its central feature a platform 'erected on the rough rock at the edge of the terrace, from which the slope drops steeply to the valley'.[34] The platform 'consisted of an elongated rampart, a small stretch of pavement, a pit and a place for burning'. It was situated in an area encircled by a seventeen-sided polygonal wall, carefully constructed in dry stone and varying in height from 1.45 m to 0.25 m (due to partial destruction). There were two entrances to the enclosure by means of steps built actually over the wall, one of which leads directly to the platform. In a spot just below the platform was 'an area full of burnt debris, charcoal pieces, burnt animal bones, and black earth saturated with fat; even the stones found there were blackened . . . fragments of the cooking pot were found . . . immediately below the burnt spot'.[35] 'The place was thus prepared for ritual acts, the nature of which escapes us. Only one feature seems definitely to have been part of that rite, namely the burning of some sort of organic material; this activity may have been either cooking or sacrificing.'[36]

At a later stage in its existence the whole site, including the enclosure wall, was covered with a huge heap of loose fieldstones, which formed an enormous cone-shaped 'tumulus' 6 m in height and 32 m in diameter. The other tumuli examined all contained similar features beneath a pile of stones. There was no sign of a burial associated with any of the tumuli. The subsequent covering of each site with a heap of stones seems to indicate a deliberate attempt (? during Josiah's reforms) to desecrate a cultic site.[37]

Summary

Although the dates at which these various structures were built range over a wide period – from chalcolithic (En-Gedi) to the seventh century B.C. ('Tumuli') – certain characteristic features emerge:

i. A bamah is a man-made structure, built of loose fieldstones carefully packed together.
ii. In shape it is round, tapering towards the top, giving the appearance of a truncated cone; the top was a flat platform.
iii. It could be of very considerable size: up to 14 m in base diameter.
iv. The top could be reached by a flight of steps.
v. The whole structure was situated within a walled enclosure which might also (though not necessarily) include a roofed building.
vi. The bamah itself was open to the sky.
vii. It was situated on a natural eminence in open country near a settlement, or on high ground within a city.
viii. It is often associated with burnt animal bones and/or remains of fat or oil, and so appears to have been used as an altar.
ix. There is no evidence that any of them was associated with a burial.
x. A site once marked by a bamah shows a tendency to continue as a sacred place through several centuries: either the ancient bamah was retained (or restored) despite surrounding alterations, or a new structure was built – but on the same spot.

It is remarkable that practically every one of these characteristics can be paralleled from the Old Testament passages already cited.

TYPE II BAMOTH

Excavations have laid bare another type of structure, several examples of which may be noted. Each is a low, straight-sided, platform, found in an unmistakably cultic context, and one where no conical bamah (as described above) is present. I postulate that these are examples of a second type of bamah. As far as possible the descriptions below follow the excavators' own words.

Hazor

The first to be identified was found at Hazor,[38] dating from the period immediately prior to the destruction of the city in the thirteenth century B.C. Our structure is one item in a temple complex, consisting of a large open court surrounded by a series of rooms.

Y. Yadin says it ‘seems to have had a cult function. It is a sort of elevated rectangular platform, without connection with the surrounding buildings, and is placed at the end of the Square. The objects found on it . . . which included cooking pots, a baking tray and a bull's skull – strengthen the belief that this structure was used in the cult.’[39] ‘Its preserved length is 6.50 m . . . its interior is patchily paved with stone, mostly large flat slabs. The structure is on the average 0.60 m higher than its surroundings.’[40] Although in the final report this structure is non-commitally called a ‘Cult Place’, Yadin himself had earlier described it as a bamah.[41]

A second structure officially described as a ‘Cult Place’[42] was found in another temple at Hazor. In a preliminary report[43] Yadin describes how this temple had two adjacent courts, the first of which served as an entrance porch. ‘In front of this entrance was a spacious cobbled open court, with a fairly large rectangular *bamah* or altar, and several small altars.’ Photographs[42] show the bamah to be a low, free-standing platform, with straight sides, built up with uncut stones of varying sizes on the cobbled floor.

Tell Arad

What seems to be a similar example of a straight-sided bamah has recently been found at Tell Arad, dating from about 2900–2700 B.C. Full details are not yet available, as the final excavation report has not yet been published. But a preliminary report[44] describes how 'a building of great size was found' inside the acropolis, which 'had a hall (*salle*) with two monolith columns and the base of a third. Outside and close to this building was found a square platform made of large stones. The hall and platform are apparently a temple.' This sounds suspiciously like the platforms at Hazor.

Arad may possibly provide yet another example of a straight-sided bamah, this time from the tenth century B.C., in a temple apparently used for Yahweh worship. Again only preliminary reports are available at present.[45] One of these describes how 'inside the *debir* was a small, square, paved *bamah* and, beside it, a fallen *maṣṣebah*'.[46] Once again one feels cautious about accepting Aharoni's ready identification of a *bamah*. The accompanying photograph shows it to be a tiny platform in the very corner of the *debir*-room, raised only a few inches above the surrounding floor level. No archaeological evidence is given to show to what purpose this little platform was put. Would it be better described as an offering table? But a more important criticism of this identification is that no other bamah is known to have been built *inside* a room; all others are open to the sky.

Tel Dan

More recently (1970), a bamah of monumental size and style of construction has been discovered at Tel Dan – almost certainly the bamah built by Jeroboam I. 'In the centre of the area [Area T] an almost square structure was revealed, measuring 18.2 × 18.7 m, whose outer walls were of dressed limestone . . . the width of the walls varied between 1.5 to 2.3 m. The building method was uniform, the two lower courses were of headers whilst the upper courses were laid in headers and stretchers. All the stones were dressed in the style characteristic of the period of the Israelite monarchy. In some places the walls were preserved to a height of about 1.5 m in all, though. It was impossible to determine the original height of the structure. The space enclosed by the four walls was filled with basalt stones forming a wide, flat platform.

'On the southern edge of the *bama*, facing the town, an 8 m wide monumental flight of steps was uncovered, built directly against the outer wall of the *bama* . . . Pottery collected from the steps point to a date in the mid-9th century B.C. The *bama*, first erected in the MBA II, was enlarged in the following generations.'[47] (See plates 2(a) and 2(b).)

Shechem

For the sake of completeness, mention must also be made of a straight-sided platform-like structure found at the lowest level (*ca.* 1800 B.C.) of Shechem. Maybe this is another oblong bamah; but incomplete excavation makes certain identification impossible.[48]

PLATFORMS AS BASES TO ALTARS

There are several instances of low platforms such as those just described having altars built on them – in other words serving as altar bases.

Shechem

A good example was found at Shechem, where a succession of temples existed over a period of seven centuries. These successive temples were orientated on differing axes, but all had a common fulcrum – the site of the altar, which in each case remained constant.

For our present purposes the significant feature is the brick base which was carefully built for the altar of Fortress Temple I^b. 'In size its reddish bricks were 35 to 43 cm square, and these were evidently surmounted by a low curb made of white marl bricks, *ca.* 35 cm square.[49] . . . This is *ca.* 3.50 m ($11\frac{1}{2}$ ft) long.'[50] The layer overlying the bricks is 'unique among the fills found in the temple courtyard, a thick deposit of *huwwar* chips with very little earth among them . . . The chips probably functioned as the interior composition of a larger structure of which the brick layers are the foundation. The location in front of the temple would indicate that the brick structure was the basement of an altar composed of a compact mass of *huwwar* chips consolidated and held in place by a layer of plaster, some fragments of which are still preserved.'[51]

We thus have a rectangular platform about the same height as the Hazor ones, situated in a temple courtyard as at Hazor. In addition, this platform is known to have had an altar built on it.[52] Both structures were very carefully made (though the material differs), and both had a deliberate curb edging.

Petra

Another example of an altar positioned on a low platform-base is that at the Great High Place (the 'Robinson' High Place) at Petra. In common with the tradition of Petra, the whole of this sanctuary is rock-cut: nothing is built. The sanctuary consists of a large rectangular court, with a level floor cut into the mountain-top. Immediately outside its west side stands a rectangular altar. It also is cut out of solid rock, a space being left to walk all round it. What is significant is that the level to which the floor around the altar has been cut is one step higher than the level of the adjacent court. Is this because an altar of this sort needed to have a low platform-base? The manner in which the rest of the sanctuary has been constructed (with such careful attention being paid to the levelling of the floor of the court) makes it impossible to suppose that the level of the floor around the altar is merely fortuitous.[53]

Tell Arad

A third possible example of a low platform-base to an altar may occur at Tell Arad. As already stated the full excavation report is unfortunately not yet available; but from the photographs and preliminary reports of Y. Aharoni[54] certain tentative points may be made. Situated in the large open court of the Stratum x temple is a holocaust altar. For our present purposes the interesting feature of the altar is the step in front of it. Apparently (to judge from the photographs) it is constructed out of flat slab stones placed on top of each other to make a low step, about a foot wide and stretching along the entire length of one side of the altar. Aharoni, in passing, refers to it as 'a step in front of the altar which is a vestige of an older altar [on which] were found several offering bowls'.[55]

But is this merely a 'step'? Or is it an integral part of the altar? – its base (in this case the ancient base of an earlier altar re-used). It seems unlikely that in rebuilding the altar of Stratum x a piece of the Stratum xi altar was deliberately retained – merely to be used as a 'step'. It is much more likely that it was retained because it was an actual part (the base) of the older altar, and as such was itself holy. Aharoni himself is at pains to point out that 'the altar . . . was always rebuilt on the same spot'.[56] This parallels the rebuilding procedure at Shechem. If, then, the base of the altar was the fundamental thing (in more than one sense), is this why it was appropriate to leave offering bowls there, and not on the altar itself?[57] However, judgement on this must await publication of the final report.

Summary

The time-span of Type ii bamoth ranges from Early Bronze ii down to Hellenistic times. But the following characteristics emerge:

i. The bamah can be constructed in stone or brick, in some cases careful attention being paid to the curb edges.
ii. In shape it is rectangular or square, giving the appearance of a low platform, one or more steps above the surrounding ground level.
iii. Known examples can be up to 18 m long, and 1.5 m in height, although much smaller ones seem common.
iv. It is found only inside rather elaborate temples.
v. The bamah itself was open to the sky (with one possible exception).
vi. It was used as an altar: either offerings could be placed directly on the bamah, or more often the bamah seems to have served the purpose of being the base for a rectangular altar built upon it.

In addition it should be noted that a Type II bamah never occurs in conjunction with a Type I bamah. Type II may therefore be regarded as a stylised form of the primitive bamah, more suited to the sophisticated temples in which they stand.

It will have become clear from this discussion that a direct relation is being made between the term bamah and the base of a holocaust altar. Can such an interpretation of the archaeological finds be justified? Only literary material can give evidence in a matter of terminology, and to this we now turn.

LITERARY EVIDENCE FOR TYPE II BAMOTH

Of all the Biblical passages referring to altars, that in Ezekiel xliii is the most detailed, and it is here that mention is made of the base platform to an altar. Verses 13–17 describe the structure of Ezekiel's visionary altar for the future sanctuary. Though his vision was never actually enacted, the details clearly reflect existing patterns. Indeed it is not impossible that his description is based on knowledge and memory of the ancient Solomonic altar.[58]

Ezekiel describes the altar as being composed of three cubes of diminishing size placed on top of each other, the topmost being capped with 'horns' at the four corners – all very reminiscent of a Mesopotamian ziggurat.[59] The whole altar rests on a low platform-base. This is 1 cubit high, and provides a plinth 1 cubit wide around the lowest of the three cubes. It is edged with a curb 1 span wide. The relation of this base to the altar-platforms described in the previous section is thus very close, right down to such details as the curb.

The word Ezekiel uses for the base is a technical one: *ḥêq*. Some commentators, taking the word in its more common sense of 'breast, lap', think of the base as a hollow structure *into* which the altar fitted.[60] The conception of the base as a raised platform thus tends to get lost.

But it is clear that *ḥêq*, particularly in its full form *ḥêq hā'āreṣ*, 'bosom of the earth' (verse 14), is a technical term for the base platform of a sacred structure. An expression with precisely the same meaning – *irat erṣiti* – is used by Nebuchadrezzar in his inscriptions for the foundation-platform of the royal palace and the great temple-tower of Marduk in Babylon. This surprising link with Akkadian usage is confirmed by the fact that the name Ezekiel gives to the topmost section of his altar also has an Akkadian parallel.[61] (In any case there is a likelihood of Mesopotamian connections because of the altar's shape, as mentioned above.) This evidence supports the suggestion that the *ḥêq* was visualised as being raised *above* the surrounding ground level.

Has this base-platform any connection with a Type II bamah? Once again the significance of Ezekiel's description has been largely missed. At the end of verse 13, after he has given the measurements of the *ḥêq* and its curb, he says: *w^e zeh gaḇ hammizbēaḥ* (LXX: καὶ τοῦτο τὸ ὕψος τοῦ θυσιαστηρίου).

Most commentators are influenced by the LXX rendering of *gaḇ*,[62] emend it to *gōḇah*, and take the phrase as the opening of the next verse – 'Now this is the *height* of the altar . . .' But there is independent evidence to show that the LXX did not understand Ezekiel's use of *gaḇ*,[63] and so its witness should not be relied upon here.

It is however quite possible to take the MT as it stands, since Ezekiel uses *gaḇ* as a virtual synonym for *bāmâ* in xvi 24, 31, 39.[64] The primary meaning *gaḇ* seems to be something akin to 'hump/mound'.[65] It therefore commonly occurs in the construct state, followed by a noun which describes what sort of 'hump/mound' is intended. This is precisely how it occurs in xliii 13 – *hammizbēaḥ* functioning in an adjectival capacity indicating 'altar-mound'. The phrase *wᵉzeh gaḇ hammizbēaḥ* may thus be a note equating a new term (*ḥêq hā'āreṣ*) and an ancient term (*gaḇ*). The end of verse 13 should perhaps therefore be translated:

> Its foundation platform shall be one cubit high and one cubit broad, with a curb of one span around its edge. This is the 'mound' for the altar.

However, whether or not the *ḥêq* be thought of as being sunk into the ground, or above surrounding ground level, it is clear that it was the base-platform on which the whole altar stood. As already stated, there are strong indications that the altar of Ezekiel's vision was not unique, but represented a known (and possibly common) type of altar built on a platform.

Further evidence for such altar-platforms is provided by the Greek word βωμός. Its relation to *bāmâ* and its probable non-Greek origin have already been noted. It meant not only 'altar' but also 'altar-platform'. Words derived from it suggest a plinth structure with a low oblong shape.[66] In other words, the fundamental concept behind the cultic use of βωμός was not merely 'altar', but an altar of a particular shape: one raised on an oblong platform. Surviving remains of early Greek altars in fact show that they were either built on a platform, or were themselves a platform. In view of the increasing evidence of Semitic influence on all levels of early Greek culture, it is likely that these altars reflect designs current at the time the word βωμός was borrowed.

SUMMARY OF CONCLUSIONS

bāmâ seems to be derived from a non-extant noun conveying the general concept of 'rib-cage, middle-of-the-body, flank'.

In our extant Hebrew texts it occurs with three groups of derived meanings:

i. topographical senses: 'hill-sides', and possibly 'grave-mound';

ii. anatomical senses: 'backs', and possibly 'beast';

iii. cultic senses: 'cultic platform', and by extension 'altar' and 'sanctuary'.

Two types of cultic platforms (bamoth) have been found in excavations: truncated cones of some height; and low oblong ones which may also have had an altar standing on them.

All attempts to find an etymological link between the cultic and secular senses of *bāmâ* have so far failed. Recent work on Akkadian and Ugaritic cognates widens rather than closes the gap between the two senses. It seems probable therefore that an etymological link does not exist. The cultic sense of *bāmâ* was coined within the context of a cultic mythology about Yahweh 'treading upon *bāmᵒṯê 'āreṣ*'.

At no point is there any evidence of a cult of the dead being associated with bamoth.

ABBREVIATIONS OF NAMES OF BIBLICAL BOOKS USED IN THE NOTES

Am	Amos
Ch	Chronicles
Dt	Deuteronomy
Ex	Exodus
Ezk	Ezekiel
Gn	Genesis
Hab	Habakkuk
Ho	Hosea
Is	Isaiah
Jb	Job
Jg	Judges
Jos	Joshua
Jr	Jeremiah
K	Kings
Lv	Leviticus
M	Maccabees
Mi	Micah
Nb	Numbers
Ps	Psalms
S	Samuel
Si	Ecclesiasticus

NOTES TO INTRODUCTION AND CHAPTER I (pp. 1–28)

1. This is in part a rebuttal of certain views of L. H. Vincent put forward in two lengthy articles entitled 'La Notion Biblique du Haut-Lieu', *RB* LV (1948), pp. 245–78 and 438–45. Vincent attempted to give a comprehensive picture of the Biblical usage of *bāmâ* in relation to archaeological evidence as it then was. A major part of his first article is taken up with a discussion of the Gezer sanctuary, which he took to be a typical bamah. Much of this discussion now seems irrelevant to study of bamoth, in the light of further archaeological developments. But many of Vincent's insights regarding the Biblical usage of the word *bāmâ* remain valid. Vincent in turn was expanding on Albright's earlier discussion of bamoth in *ARI*^{2} (1946), pp. 105–7. The latter was probably the first comprehensive (though brief) attempt to survey the new archaeological and philological evidence in relation to the Biblical text.
2. The distribution of the word throughout the Old Testament is as follows: Lv 1, Nb 2, Dt 2, S 10, K 39, Ch 19, Jb 1, Ps 2, Is 5, Jr 6, Ezk 7, Ho 1, Am 2, Mi 3, Hab 1. These figures are based on S. Mandelkern, *Veteris Testamenti Concordiae* . . . (Schocken, Tel Aviv, 1969). See also the concordance appendixed to this monograph.
3. The commonest LXX rendering is the adjective 'high' with the neuter article – τό ὑψηλόν. What noun is to be understood with the adjective is never stated (? χωρίον). Thus the problem, as to what sort of a 'high thing' a bamah was, is continually evaded by the LXX translators. In a few places, however, they clearly understood *bāmâ* to be a technical term, and rendered it by the transliteration βαμα. A full discussion of the LXX understanding of *bāmâ* is given on pages 33–5.
4. This was the supposed verbal root assumed by V. Schindler, *Lexicon Pentaglotton* (Hanover, 1612), and accepted by such other lexicographers as J. D. Michaelis, *Supplementa ad Lexica Hebraica* (Göttingen, 1792), W. Gesenius, *A Hebrew Lexicon to the Books of the Old Testament*, trans. C. Leo (Cambridge, 1825) and thence into *BDB*, which has been the basis of all but the most recent discussion of the subject. As late as 1956, W. F. Albright, *ARI*, p. 202, note 24, was using בום as the basis for his etymology of *bāmâ*. He saw the medial ו as being preserved in the Greek form βωμός. Much earlier, J. D. Michaelis, *Supplementa*, had wondered whether *bāmâ* might not have been derived from βωμός, creeping into Hebrew through Greek commerce with the Phoenicians – 'Suspicior ergo exoticum esse, a βωμὸς, atque ut pauca alia Graeca in linguam Phoenicum, id vero est, Hebraicum, commerciis Phoenicum cum Graecis immigrasse'.
5. Perhaps the most exotic attempt to establish the etymology of *bāmâ* from a verbal root בום comes in J. Fuerst, *A Hebrew and Chaldee Lexicon*, trans. S. Davidson (London, 1871). The article reads, 'בּוּם (not used) *intr.* properly *to be bellied, thick*, thence *to be high* (e.g. by heaping up) . . . The organic root בָּם is cognate with the stems פָּאֵם Ar. فَخُمَ فَعُمَ *to be thick, to be large in circumference* ... the idea of height in בָּמָה is a farther development of this fundamental significance'!
6. *KB*^{1} (1953) dropped any reference to a root בום, while W. F. Albright, *HPAP* (1957), pp. 255f., posited an original pre-Semitic noun **bahmat*. This has been accepted by R. de Vaux, *AI*, p. 284 and many others

since, and is now included in the etymology of *bāmâ* in *KB*³ (1967). H. Torczyner, *Bulletin of the Jewish Palestine Exploration Society*, III (1933), pp. 9–18, had likewise abandoned a verbal root, and proposed that *bāmâ* was the equivalent of Akkadian *bamtu*, and so means 'stomach, centre'. But this fails to satisfy all the Biblical usages of *bāmâ*.

7. W. F. Albright, *JPOS*, XIV (1934), p. 120, note 86; C. H. Gordon, *Ugaritic Grammar* (Rome, 1940), p. 95*b* and *Ugaritic Textbook* (Rome, 1965), p. 373; and now *KB*³, in article בָּמָה.
8. M. Held, 'Studies in Comparative Semitic Lexicography', in H. G. Güterbock and T. Jacobsen (eds.), *Studies in Honor of Benno Landsberger* (Chicago, 1965), p. 406.
9. The translation here and below is based on that of H. L. Ginsberg in *ANET*, pp. 129ff.
10. 5 (I*AB) vi 20–2, *CTCA*, p. 36.
11. 6 (I AB) i 4–5, *CTCA*, p. 38.
12. Held suggests that the frequent sequence in Akkadian diagnostic texts of *reš libbi* and *ṣēlu* corroborate that *bmt* is here a virtual synonym for *'ap lb*.
13. 3 (V AB) B 11–13, *CTCA*, p. 15.
14. 4 (II AB) iv–v 14–15, *CTCA*, p. 25.
15. 19 (I D) 59–60, *CTCA*, p. 88.
16. C. Virolleaud, *Le Palais Royal d'Ugarit*, vol. II (Paris, 1957), p. 162, no. 128, l. 17.
17. Virolleaud takes *bmt* to mean 'backbones' (*échines*), no doubt influenced by the usual interpretation of *bmt* as 'back'. If the sense 'carcase/rib-cage' be accepted, *bmt* in this line then stands in sharp contrast to the previous item listed: *sl't.'alp.mr'e* 'ribs of a fat ox' – i.e. a whole carcase as distinct from the few 'chops' of the previous item.
18. 4 (II AB) vii 34–5, *CTCA*, p. 29.
19. After Gaster, Aistleitner, *Untersuchungen*, p. 114, and accepted by G. R. Driver, *Canaanite Myths and Legends* (Edinburgh, 1956), p. 100.
20. Three of the factors calling for caution are: (i) *'arṣ* does not satisfactorily fill out the probable gap of four letters after *'a*. (ii) The verb *nṯṯ* 'to wobble' is elsewhere only used with a personal subject – of the feet wobbling ('one of the signs of physical collapse on getting bad news'; see Gordon, *Ugaritic Textbook*, p. 395, no. 1641). (iii) It is doubtful procedure to supply wanting letters which create a unique expression in Ugaritic, which in turn can only be interpreted in the light of a Hebrew idiomatic phrase!
21. Since Ugaritic has more common words for 'back' (which are never used in synonymous parallelism with *bmt*), it is not unlikely that *bmt* will refer to some other part of human and animal anatomy. Gordon, *Ugaritic Textbook*, p. 421, classifies *ksl* as meaning 'the back'. But Held, 'Studies', pp. 405f., claims that *ksl* properly means 'sinew', and that 'back' is only a secondary meaning, the sequence being sinew > sinew of the back > back. 'The word for back in Ugaritic', he claims, 'is neither *ksl* nor *bmt*... but rather *ẓr*' (p. 406; see especially note 150 for full references to *ẓr* = 'back').
22. *CAD*, 2, pp. 78f., art. *bamtu* B, from which the following quotations are taken, and where full references may be found.
23. Held, 'Studies', has pointed out that this text is the clearest possible evidence that in Canaanite *bmt* did not mean 'back'. The scribe has

specifically explained the Akkadian word here with the gloss *baṭnuma*, 'belly', in contradistinction from *zuḫrūma*, 'back'.

24. *CAD*, 16, pp. 124f. References show that *ṣēlu* can mean either a single rib, or the whole rib-cage.

25. W. von Soden, *Akkadisches Handwörterbuch*, vol. I (Wiesbaden, 1959–65), p. 101*b*, art. *bāmtu*(*m*). All three senses, 'middle', '(mountain-)slope', and 'area of the ribs' (=*CAD*'s *bamtu* A, *bamâtu*, and *bamtu* B respectively), are treated as belonging to a single root.

26. Is xiv 14; Am iv 13; Jb ix 8. Also written במותי in Dt xxxii 13, Is lviii 14 and Mi i 3, but the Massorah corrects these to conform with the previous three cases. In all six cases, the word is pointed בָּמֳתֵי. For discussion of this peculiar form see *GK*, 87.s and 95.o.

27. *drk* is the verb most frequently associated with *bāmᵒṯê*, occurring in Dt xxxiii 29; Am iv 13; Mi i 3; Jb ix 8; and Hab iii 19. *rkb* occurs in Dt xxxii 13, and Is lviii 14, while *'lh* is used in Is xiv 14, and *'md* in 2 S xxii 34 = Ps xviii 34.

28. M. H. Pope, *Job* (Garden City, 1965), p. 70, suggests that 'treading on high places . . . represents the victorious avenger trampling the backs of the wicked earth'. He notes the Mesopotamian myths about the primeval battle which resulted in separation of Earth and Sea. But in neither Mesopotamian nor Hebrew mythology is Earth an enemy. It is Sea who is defeated. On the other hand, the idea of walking on land in order to claim ownership of it is prominent in the OT, e.g. Dt xi 24 'every place on which the sole of your foot treads shall be yours' (cf. also Gn xiii 17; Dt i 36, xi 25; Jos xiv 9; Mi v 4–5). It is possible that the idea of Yahweh treading on *bāmᵒṯê 'ereṣ* is related to the concept behind the rock-reliefs of Yazilikaya, where some gods are represented as walking upon mountains as well as upon beasts (cf. E. Laroche, 'Le Pantheon de Yazilikaya', *Journal of Cuneiform Studies*, VI (1952), pp. 115–23).

29. Dt xxxii 13, xxxiii 29; 2 S i 19, 25; Is xiv 14, lviii 14; Am iv 13; Mi i 3; Jb ix 8. As their contexts show, 2 S xxii 34 = Ps xviii 34, and Hab iii 19 must also be reckoned as examples of the same poetic formula. The peculiar MT בָּמֳתַי (rationalised by LXX and *BH*^{3} to בָּמוֹת) may be original. A. Sperber, *A Historical Grammar of Biblical Hebrew* (Leiden, 1966), p. 40, accepts it as a plural absolute. M. Dahood, *Psalms I* (Garden City, 1966), p. 115, accepts it for a different reason – as a perfectly correct archaic third person suffix. This is attractive, as 'upon *his* (mountain-) slopes he makes me stand/ride' fits the context so well. If this is correct, together with Dt xxxiii 29 and 2 S i 19, 25, these are suffixed forms of בָּמֳתֵי, Other suffixed forms בָּמֹתָיו (2 K xviii 22 = Is xxxvi 7 = 2 Ch xxxii 12), בָּמוֹתֵיכֶם (Lv xxvi 30; Ezk vi 3) and בָּמוֹתָם (Nb xxxiii 52; Ps lxxviii 58; and ?Ezk xliii 7) must be regarded as suffixed forms of בָּמוֹת, and have a cultic meaning (as their contexts make clear). The distinction between בָּמוֹתֵימוֹ (Dt xxxiii 29) and בָּמוֹתָם is thus a significant one.

30. Failure to recognise this has confused most discussions of *bāmâ*. The confusion is of long standing. Schindler, *Lexicon*, for instance, gives as his first sense of *bāmâ*: *altitudo, celsitudo, excelsitas, eminentior*. No doubt he was influenced by LXX and Vulg., and by the fact that it was known from the text that bamoth were built on hills. This idea has persisted down to *BDB* and *KB*^{1} who list 'high place, mountain' and 'hills' (respectively)

as their first sense of *bāmâ*. So taken for granted is the idea of height that *bāmôt 'arnôn* (Nb xxi 28) could be translated (RSV) 'heights of Arnon' – which is a river! Vincent contributed fundamentally to the discussion of *bāmâ* when he noted: 'Il semblerait . . . que l'idée de 'hauteur' n'est pas philologiquement intrinsèque à במה' ('La Notion Biblique', p. 278). This is echoed by de Vaux: 'the idea of a mountain or hill is not contained in the world itself' (*AI*, p. 284).

31. First recognised by F. M. Cross and D. N. Freedman, 'The Blessing of Moses', *JBL* LXVII (1948), pp. 191–210, who translate: 'But thou upon their backs dost tread.' On the peculiar MT form *bāmôṯêmô*, they comment (note 93): 'The Samaritan text במתמ preserves tenth century spelling, while the Massoretic text gives the archaic poetic vocalization of the suffix. Read *'al-bmôtēmô*, for metrical reasons.' Illustrations of the practice of treading on the bodies of enemies are provided in Jos x 24; Ps cx 1, and possibly lx 12 = cviii 14, and also in Egyptian art (e.g. W. M. F. Petrie, *A History of Egypt*, vol. II^{7} (London, 1924), fig. 96, where Amenophis II is depicted with his feet on his foes).

32. This suggestion was first put forward by W. F. Albright in the course of a book review of G. Hölscher, *Das Buch Hiob* (Tübingen, 1937), in *JBL* LVII (1938), p. 227. He proposed this translation as one of 'two very fine illustrations, both new . . . of the vocabulary and the mythological allusions in Job from the Ugarit texts'. The line 'should be read as though it were in a Ugaritic context, with *bmt* meaning "back", and rendered, "and Who treads on the back of Yam".' The Ugaritic text which gives details of the battle between Baal and Yamm is III AB A 15. In this passage, Kothar makes clubs for Baal which will 'strike the back of Yamm' (*ANET*^{2}, p. 131). Jb vii 12 is a further evidence that the author of Job was familiar with a Yahweh version of this myth.

33. Viz. after defeating him. The RSV, following the majority of commentators, translates *bām^{o}ṯê yām* as 'waves of the sea'. All who give it this meaning assume that *bām^{o}ṯê* has the sense 'heights', and that the expression 'heights of the sea' is poetic imagery for (mountainous) waves. But as has already been shown, the idea of height is not inherent in *bām^{o}ṯê*. Moreover, the context of the line is describing Yahweh's acts in creation. But God's treading on waves is nowhere else noted as one of the events of creation, whereas the defeat of Yamm/Sea most certainly is. All the evidence thus points to the sense 'body/back(s)', and this is the sense accepted by Pope (*Job*, pp. 69f.) and *NEB*. The form *bām^{o}ṯê* is obviously plural, but its meaning will probably be singular (since only one creature is being trodden on). *bām^{o}ṯê* would thus be a 'plural of local extension' (cf. *GK* §124*b*, and note 39 below). Alternatively, the meaning might be plural, referring to the many loops ('backs') of the sea-monster/serpent. But this is speculative, since we have no way of knowing what shape the monster was visualised as being.

34. Again taking *bām^{o}ṯê* as a 'plural of local extension'. The alternative is to take it with a plural meaning, and to assume *'āḇ* to be a collective singular. The former is perhaps slightly to be preferred since there is only one rider.

35. This sense is borne out by the succeeding preposition. *'lh 'al* is commonly used of ascending *on* to (not *above*) something: e.g. of ascending on to an altar by steps (Ex xx 23), on to a roof (Jos iii 18, Jg ix 51) or on to a bed (Ps cxxxii 3). An example of Yahweh being described as riding upon a cloud is Is xix 1 (cf. the same concept in Dt xxxiii 26, Ps civ 3,

and (?) lxviii 5), and this should be compared with 'Rider of the Clouds' as a common title of Baal in the Ugaritic myths.

36. So *BDB*, *KB*³, etc.

37. It is possible that the passage quoted is implying some sort of distinction between *bāmᵒṯê 'ereṣ* (mythological mountains) and *hārîm* (ordinary mountains).

38. 1 Ch xxi 29, xvi 39 and 2 Ch i 3, 13.

39. Cf. *GK* §124*b*, who comments that 'plurals of *local extension* . . . denote locations in general, but especially level surfaces'. Such a plural is thus particularly appropriate in the word *bāmâ*, for a bamah was thought of not so much as a solid structure, as a raised *surface* (platform) upon which rites were performed. Certain surfaces of the body were also used with a 'plural of local extension': thus *'aḥôrîm* is used with the singular sense 'back' in Ex xxvi 12 etc. Significantly, this seems to be the sense demanded of its synonym *bāmᵒṯê* in Jb ix 8 and Is xiv 14 and perhaps Dt xxxiii 29.

40. Cf. R. Meyer, *Hebraïsche Grammatik*³ (Berlin, 1966), vol. II, p. 39, and J. Friedrich, *Phönizische–Punische Grammatik* (Rome, 1951), p. 99, §228. Transliterations of certain names show that where Hebrew would normally have an *a*-vowel for the ending of fem. sing. abs. and constr., Phoenician had an *ō*-vowel. Thus אמת־מלקרת = *'Amōt–Milqart.*

41. It is possible that the MT has pointed incorrectly here (cf. *HPAP*, pp. 245f.). במות הַשְּׁעָרִים (RSV: 'the high places of the gates') should perhaps be pointed במות הַשְּׂעִרִים and translated 'the bamah of the demons/satyrs' (taking בְּמוֹת as singular). Cf. Lv xvii 7 where the practice of sacrificing to demons – *śᵉ'īrîm* – is mentioned. The reference to שְׂעִרִים later in the verse will doubtless account for the MT pointing of שְׁעָרִים. But whether the verse is referring to 'bamah of the gates' or 'bamah of the demons' makes no difference for our purpose: in either case a single bamah on one site is being referred to. Was this a private bamah? Cf. the small shrine found at Hazor outside the entrance to a palatial building in Area A, locus 254.

42. Jr vii 31 and xxxii 35 specifically say that the structure was built in the Valley of Hinnom. LXX, Targum and RSV assume a singular sense in vii 31, and a single structure is also implied in 2 K xxiii 10: '[Josiah] defiled *'eṯ-hattōp̄eṯ*.'

43. So J. M. P. Smith, *Micah* (*ICC*, Edinburgh, 1912), p. 34, who prefers to follow the LXX ἡ ἁμαρτία ὄικου and emends the MT to *ḥaṭṭa'ṯ*, thus maintaining the parallel with the previous couplet. G. W. Wade (*Westminster Comm*., *ad loc*.) follows the Greek even closer by inserting *bêṯ* as well, and supposes scribal misreading of the medial letter of *byt* to have produced *bmt*. RSV follows this double correction. But such a double insertion upsets the metrical balance of the line. Most commentators follow one or other of these opinions.

44. Cf. Smith, *Micah*: '[*bamot*] is impossible because the answer *Jerusalem* does not fit; nor was Jerusalem noted for *high-places*, the temple taking their place . . . the sin of Judah as Micah saw it consisted in oppression, murder, etc., rather than on worshipping on the high-places.' But, on the contrary, the whole passage is decrying the cultic impurity of Israel and Judah.

45. It has in fact been reinstated by *NEB*. A Dead Sea fragment from Cave 1 agrees with the text of the MT (see D. Barthélemy and J. T. Milik, *Discoveries in the Judean Desert*, vol. 1 (Oxford, 1955), p. 78).

46. It is of course possible that *bāmôṯ* could have a plural meaning, referring to the bamoth of the hills around Jerusalem (cf. 2 K xxiii 13). But as already noted, the parallel with *peša'* prefers a singular meaning.

47. The sense 'heights' suggested itself presumably because the whole oracle is addressed to the mountains of Israel. Others (eg. BH^3, G. A. Cooke, *Ezekiel* (*ICC*, Edinburgh, 1936), and W. Eichrodt, *Ezekiel* (London, 1970)) follow LXX ἔρημα αἰώνια. But this cannot be regarded as a reliable alternative reading to MT. What enemy would exult in possessing a 'perpetual devastation'?

48. Because of the pagan associations of the word, a Hebrew would not normally refer to the Jerusalem Temple as *bāmâ*. But in the mouth of a pagan enemy, as here, *bāmâ* is most appropriate.

49. The significance of the enemy's boast of possessing the shrine is illuminated by R. E. Clements's discussion of the close relationship between a sanctuary and its land (*God and Temple* (Oxford, 1965), Chapter 4). The enemy was boasting that by having (proleptically) taken the sanctuary, he now had a right to the whole land! It is also possible that *bāmôṯ* in this verse has a plural meaning. But it will still have a cultic sense 'sanctuaries' and will refer to the various bamoth scattered around the hills of the land.

50. Nb xxi 19, 20, 28, xxii 41; Jos xiii 17.

51. For the special relation between *bāmâ* and Moab, see the discussion in Chapter II.

52. *bāmôṯ 'arnôn* must refer to a town and not a district, since it is described as being burnt along with the cities Heshbon, Ar, Dibon and Medeba. It is unusual that the determinative of *bāmôṯ* is a geographical feature, and not the name of the god worshipped there. This may be a poetic abbreviation for the more usual and prosaic *bāmôṯ ba'al* (meaning 'bamah of Baal') of Nb xxii 41 and Jos xiii 17 – which is probably that same place. The way in which Targum Onkelos understood the phrase is perhaps significant. Not only is *bāmôṯ* taken in a cultic sense, but the phrase *ba'*^{a}*lê bāmôṯ* is taken to mean the pagan priests (*kûmrayyâ*) who served at the shrine (singular: *bêṯ dah*^{a}*lâ*) in the Arnon uplands.

53. *HPAP*, p. 245. The peculiar spelling of the word in 1Q Is^{a} will be discussed below in relation to earlier forms of *bāmâ*. It is interesting to note that in the seventeenth century V. Schindler (*Lexicon*, p. 170) considered that the word should be בָּמוֹתָיו and commented 'Idem igitur sunt קֶבֶר *sepulchrum*, & בָּמֹת *monumenta*.'

54. *HPAP*, pp. 245ff.

55. This emendation does not originate with Albright, but is of long standing, having found its way into BH^3 – of which A. Guillaume cynically remarks: 'Kittel even thinks it worth while to retain the monstrous "emendation" שעירים "satyrs"' ('A Contribution to Hebrew Lexicography', *BSOAS* XVI (1954), p. 10, note 1).

56. *HPAP*, p. 247. Curiously, Albright takes no account of the frequent Biblical references to burials and the respects which were paid to the dead, but confines himself to speculation. De Vaux, after a detailed study of these references sums up by saying: 'We conclude that the dead were honoured in the religious spirit, but that no cult was paid to them' (*AI*, p. 61). A confirmatory side-light is thrown on this conclusion by R. H. Smith, 'The Household Lamps of Palestine in Old Testament Times', *BA* XXVII (1964), pp. 11f. He shows how bowls of food and lamps have been found placed *outside* Canaanite and Ugaritic tombs after

burial. He regards this as 'an act of sympathetic magic whereby the smouldering flame of life in the deceased would be rekindled' (p. 12). But he has to admit that this practice is 'not specifically proved for the Iron Age'. This all militates against Albright's theory of a widespread cult of the dead practised at bamoth.

57. Some have argued that the 'rich' and the 'wicked' are so often equated in the Prophets that they may be regarded as synonymous here. Such reasoning has missed the point. In this passage the question at issue is what type of burial the Servant was given. According to the first part of the verse it was ignominious – 'with the wicked'; the next line will hardly have added that it was 'with the rich' – in other words a sumptuous funeral!

58. It is the reading preferred by *BH*³, and amongst recent commentators is accepted by J. L. McKenzie, *Second Isaiah* (Garden City, 1968) and C. Westermann, *Isaiah 40–66* (London, 1969).

59. Guillaume, 'A Contribution', p. 10.

60. This is the translation given by E. W. Lane, *An Arabic–English Lexicon* (London, 1863–93), p. 2230*b*, quoting the Ṣiḥah, the Q̣āmūs and the Tāj el-ʿArūs. It is accepted as the sense of the Hebrew *ʿāšîr* here by C. R. North, *The Second Isaiah* (Oxford, 1964), pp. 65 and 231, and by *NEB*.

61. Albright (*HPAP*, pp. 248f.) also saw a relation in shape between burial cairns (citing those at Serābîṭ el-Khâdim) and bamoth, but went on to imply that cultic bamoth either were burial cairns or were made in imitation of them. There are many facts which conflict with this theory: (i) several structures which can conclusively be termed bamoth have been found (they will be discussed below), but none of them contains a burial either in or near it; (ii) while burial cairns and cultic bamoth have in common a heap of stones, the shape of the heap differs according to its function – cultic bamoth had a *flat* top upon which rites were practised, but this is not the case with the cairns; (iii) the common mode of burial in both Canaan and Israel was *not* in cairns.

De Vaux (*AI*, p. 287) is nearer the mark when he says: 'these funeral mounds [i.e. those of Achan, the king of Ai and Absalom] looked exactly the same as the mounds used for worship'. He considers that the relation in shape indicates that funerary rites were practised on bamoth. Nevertheless he feels it necessary to modify this by stressing that it 'must not be pressed too far; the "high places" were destined for general purposes of worship, and funerary rites were merely one element in this worship'. I would emphasise that burial mounds heaped over three renegades is, if anything, evidence *against* rather than for such mounds being used for cultic purposes.

62. Cf. the detailed description of these sepulchres in *AI*, pp. 57f.

63. 2 S xviii 17.

64. Jos vii 26.

65. Jos viii 29, reading אל־הַפַּחַת with LXX εἰς τὸν βόθρον for the MT אל־פֶּתַח שער העיר (cf. the identical form of expression in 2 S xviii 17 וישליכו אתו...אל־הַפַּחַת). The sense demands such a reading since the city was already thoroughly destroyed (verse 28) and burial within the 'gateway space' (which is what פֶּתַח שַׁעַר always means – not 'in front of the gate') would be impossible due to the burnt rubble. It is easy to understand how an original פחת could be corrupted to פתח by trans-

position; it was then necessary to explain which פֶּתַח was intended – the פֶּתַח שער העיר which is a standard idiomatic phrase.

66. A systematic dishonouring of the king of each city is implied in Jos x 26ff. Twice we are told that 'he did to its king as he had done to the king of Jericho'. Unfortunately in our extant account of the destruction of Jericho, mention of the fate of its king has dropped out, due to the present narrative's concern with Rahab. But it is reasonable to suppose that the fate of the king of Ai is typical of all.

67. We may presume that this was a grave dug in the ground, because the body was 'thrown' into it (cf. Absalom). The Hebrew text uses the word *qibrê* to describe it, which could mean 'sepulchres'. But since Hebrew has no common synonym for *qeber*, this was the only word available, and is here used with some latitude of meaning.

68. Jr xxvi 23.

69. *AI*, p. 58.

70. Is liii 12 also refers to the Servant's death. He is said to have been 'numbered with the *pōš*^{e}*ʿîm*'. This is usually translated 'transgressors'. But the verb *pāšaʿ* can mean not only to transgress against God, but to transgress against human authority, i.e. 'to rebel' (I K xii 19; 2 K i 1, iii 5, 7, viii 22; Is i 1, etc.). Does this suggest that the Servant was thought of as dying a traitor's death, like Absalom or Uriah?

71. *HPAP*, p. 246. Albright points out that there is no need to emend further to בְּבָמוֹת for בְּ is often omitted (? to avoid cacophony) before a word beginning with ב. But Albright's translation fails to meet the demands of the context at one crucial point. The whole emphasis of the passage is on the ignominious end of the wicked man and his posterity. But is the author of Job likely to have been so sectarian as to have considered it a disaster to be buried in *pagan* graves, rather than in some more respectable, orthodox, graves? Pope, *Job*, pp. 172f., senses this difficulty. He accepts the emendation *bāmôṯ* ('a cultic term for tomb or funerary monument'), but notes, 'It is still necessary to supply the negative in order to obtain sense', and so translates: 'His posterity will not be buried in tombs' (p. 169).

72. *HPAP*, p. 247.

73. Much of Albright's theory rests on D. Neiman's article '*PGR*, a Canaanite Cult-Object in the Old Testament' (*JBL* LXVII (1948), pp. 55–60), where he suggests that *peger* can mean 'stele'. Neiman's conclusions have been widely accepted, for example by de Vaux (*AI*, p. 58), although he finds the conclusion in conflict with the known data of funerary monuments of the period; and by H. G. May (with qualifications) in his commentary on Ezk xliii 7 in the *Interpreter's Bible*, but without due regard for the arbitrary reasoning behind it.

The following remarks attempt to point out how speculative are some of the assumptions underlying Neiman's and Albright's conclusions. Neiman based his suggestion on two dedicatory stone stelae found beside the Temple of Dagan at Ras Shamra, in whose Ugaritic inscriptions the word *pgr* occurs. The two inscriptions in question are translated by C. H. Gordon, *Ugaritic Literature* (Rome, 1949), p. 108, texts 69 and 70, as follows:–

'The stela (*skn*) that Tryl erected to Dagân. A monument (*pgr*) (commemorating) [a head of small] and a head of large cattle as food'

'The monument (*pgr*) that 'zn erected to Dagân, his master, (commemorating) [a head of small and a head of large] cattle in the *mḫrt* (= temple refectory ?).'

Neiman rightly notes that the first word in each inscription must be close in meaning; and since *skn* can elsewhere be shown to mean 'stele' in Ugaritic, he takes this as also the meaning of *pgr*; and so he translates Ezk xliii 7:

'With the stelae of their kings (they desecrated) their high places.' This translation is based on the curious assumption that bamoth were always acceptable places for Yahweh worship, and had only been made unholy by the borrowed Canaanite objects placed on them. But this view is clearly contradicted in the Book of Ezekiel itself. In the first place, however bamoth may have been regarded in early Israel, Ezekiel consistently regards them as pagan (vi 3, 6, xvi 16, xx 29). Secondly, Chapter xliii is not concerned with bamoth in general (all round the land), but with the Temple mount alone. Building on Neiman's work, Albright affirms: 'It is now certain from Ugaritic that the word *péger* meant not only "corpse" but also "funerary stele"' (*HPAP*, p. 247). This assertion is presumably based on his earlier observations on the two dedicatory stelae: 'These stelae cannot well be explained except as connected somehow with the prospective funerals of the persons whose names they bear' (*ARI*, p. 203, note 30). This statement is at best inconclusive, and at worst unconvincing, as the stelae so obviously stress details of the sacrifice rather than of the donor. The alternative of a non-funerary interpretation of the stelae, as given by Dussaud in the original publication of the inscriptions, may still stand: 'Elles [the stelae] concernent la fondation d'un sacrifice de la communion lors d'une fête du dieu Dagon' (R. Dussaud, *Syria* XVI (1935), p. 179).

It is hardly adequate to claim that 'like *nefeš* "breath, soul, life", which means "mortuary stela" in Aramaic inscriptions, *peger* had earlier developed the same sense' (*ARI*, p. 203, note 29). Is *nefeš* (soul) really an equivalent concept to *peger* (corpse)? And is it true that 'the Ezekiel passage may be elucidated' by the stelae found at the Byblos or Hazor sanctuaries (*HPAP*, p. 248)? Is there any evidence that they were described by the word *pgr*? Do we know why the Hazor stelae were erected anyway?

We may add that Lv xxvi 30, which Neiman and Albright claim is another instance where Hebrew *peger* means 'stele', is quite self-explanatory without recourse to altering the usual sense of 'corpse'. There is indeed a play on words in the verse – but not (as Neiman suggests) with a pun. In the general desolation which the context is describing, the bamoth will be destroyed and defiled by having men's corpses thrown over the idol-images, which are themselves sarcastically termed 'corpses' (because of their lifelessness). Such a method of desecration is used in 2 K xxiii 16, 20, and in Ezk vi 5 (where the very word *peger* is a parallel to *ḥālāl*).

74. The textual evidence for omitting *bāmôṯām* is strong (cf *BH*³: 'prb dl'). Two verses later the expression 'their harlotry and the corpses (*p̄iḡrê*) of their kings' is repeated word for word as in verse 7, *but lacking bāmôṯām*. It seems likely that the word is an insertion stemming from a corrupted dittography of the following word *beṯittām*. The versions give clear evidence that the text was in a confused state at an early date (at least twenty Hebrew MSS, Theodotion and the Targum reading *bemôṯām* 'when they died'; and LXX apparently reading *beṯôḵām* 'in their midst'). *bāmôṯām* of the MT would thus seem to be the attempt of yet another textual tradition to produce a known word out of the corruption.

75. καὶ τὸ ὄρος τοῦ οἴκου ὡς ἄλσος δρυμοῦ. Ἄλσος is nowhere else used to translate *bāmâ*, but is the usual translation of *'ašērâ*. Realising that 'high places of a wood' was not good sense, the translators temporised by keeping 'wood', and transferring for 'high places' the only cultic item which they knew to be wooden – the Asherah!
76. So RSV and virtually all commentators.
77. An emendation suggested long ago by W. Rudolph, *Jeremia* (*Handbuch zum Alten Testament*, Tübingen, 1947), p. 144, *ad* Jr xxvi 18. Rudolph, however, does not attempt to explain the omitted *h*.
78. D. R. Hillers, *Treaty-Curses and the Old Testament Prophets* (Rome, 1964) (*Biblia et Orientalia*, no. 16), pp. 53f.
79. This was first noted by M. Dahood, 'Hebrew–Ugaritic Lexicography – 1', *Biblica* XLIV (1963), p. 302. He based his remarks on Albright's brief allusion in *HPAP*, p. 256 ('Albright's discussion of the relationship between *bmt* and *bhmt* is basic'). Apparently quite independently D. R. Ap-Thomas reached the same conclusion (without reference to Albright and Dahood) in 'Two Notes on Isaiah', *Essays in Honour of Griffithes Wheeler Thatcher 1863–1950*, ed. E. C. B. MacLaurin (Sydney, 1967), pp. 45–61.
80. √*ḥšb* is most frequently found with acc. of direct object, and *lᵉ*- with indirect object. *kᵉ*- with indirect object is also found with Niphal. It is grammatically possible that *bammeh* contains a *bᵉ*- of price (cf. *GK* §119*p*). But the context makes this unlikely. For the question 'for how much can man be bought?' implies the answer 'not even for an infinite amount' – whereas the context is emphasising man's worthlessness. The idea of God acquiring man by purchase in any case is unlikely here.
81. Ap-Thomas ('Two Notes') observes that this reading is not without ancient precedent. It seems that in the early centuries of this era there was a textual tradition which read *bāmâ*. Thus there is a comment in the Babylonian Talmud about this passage, 'Read not *bammeh* but *bammah* (*sic*)' (*Zeraim* 14*a*); and Jerome insisted on translating it '*excelsus*'.
82. 'Divine breath' rendering *nᵉšāmâ* – a word used exclusively of the breath of God and the breath which God has breathed into man. It is the thing which distinguishes man from the rest of creation, and thus contrasts powerfully with 'beast' in the following line. Cf. T. C. Mitchell, 'The Old Testament Use of NᵉŠĀMÂ', *VT* XI (1961), pp. 177–87.
83. Precisely the same sentiment and construction occurs in Jb xviii 3: 'Why are we counted as beasts? (*maddûaʿ neḥšabnû kabbᵉhēmâ*).'
84. First suggested by Albright in a brief remark (*HPAP*, p. 256), but unsupported by any of the evidence given above. At the same time he posited a relation between *bāmâ* and various other words containing the radicals *bhm*; these will be discussed below.
85. *BDB* implies a connection with the Arabic verb *bhm* IV 'to shut', X 'to be dumb'. Such a connection is extremely dubious. Animals are not mute, and whereas we may speak of 'dumb animals', there is no evidence that the Semite of antiquity held such a concept. *KB*³ traces no etymology for *bᵉhēmâ* (apart from noting the obvious Arabic cognates *bahmat*, *bahīmat*, *bihām*).
86. Cf. 1 K v 13 and Gn vi 7. It will be observed that the type of creature described by the word *bᵉhēmâ* does in fact have a large 'flank'. This may explain the curious plural form in Jb xl 15 etc. – again a 'plural of local extension' (cf. note 39), used in relation to a creature with very extensive 'flanks'.

87. *HPAP*, p. 245. The references (which Albright does not gives) are: Is xv 2, xvi 12, xxxvi 7, all without *waw*; xiv 14, liii 9 (which is included in his count) and lviii 14, all with *waw*. At the same time, Albright notes a seventh occurrence of *bāmâ* (without *waw*) in Isaiah – vi 13, which he claims is preserved in 1Q Is[a], reading *bmh* for MT *bm* (cf. S. Iwry, 'MAṢṢĒBĀH and BĀMĀH in 1Q Isaiah[a] 6[13]', *JBL* LXXVI (1957), pp. 225–32, who has also 'discovered' *bāmâ* in this 1Q Is[a] reading). This emendation has been widely accepted as making some sense out of a very confused text. But this 'discovery' is by no means established. J. Sawyer, 'The Qumran Reading of Isaiah 6, 13', *Annual of the Swedish Theological Institute* III (1964), pp. 111–13, has rightly emphasised that the scribe who wrote the Qumran scroll deliberately separated *bmh* from the previous word (*mṣbt*) by a long gap, thus indicating that *bmh* begins a new phrase, and is not to be construed with *mṣbt*. What may be intended by the scroll is not בָּמָה at all, but some phrase-opener like בַּמֶּה 'where?'. In addition we may note the unlikely character of the metaphor produced by Albright's reading. Is a desecrated bamah a natural point of comparison with the destruction of the nation?

88. It has no satisfactory etymology in Greek. *LSJ*'s proposed derivation from βαίνω is unconvincing in view of the disparate meanings of the two words. It may therefore be assumed to be a borrowed foreign word, whose ending has been assimilated to the class of noun ending in accented -μός (cf. L. Meyer, *Handbuch der Griechische Etymologie* (Leipzig, 1901–2), vol. III, p. 110.

89. The parallel between βωμός and *bāmâ* has long been recognised. The LXX made use of it (see next chapter); both Schindler (*Lexicon*) and Michaelis (*Supplementa*) commented on it. Albright first discussed it in *ARI*, p. 202, note 24, when he was arguing that the root of *bāmâ* was *bûm*. However, the connection with βωμός still stands with his revised root *bhmt*. The Phoenician word had either already lost its medial *h* by the time the Greeks borrowed it, or the *h* disappeared in the process of being adopted into Greek. See the fuller discussion of βωμός in the next chapter.

90. *HPAP*, p. 245. We may add that the memory of this *h* seems to be preserved in the Massoretic pointing of the inflected forms of *bāmâ*: the long syllable *bā-* is retained at all times, contrary to the normal formation.

91. Dt xxxii 13 and Is lviii 14.

92. *HPAP*, p. 242.

93. *AI*, p. 284.

94. *HPAP*, *passim*, and especially pp. 255f.

95. The reference he cites is '[E. W.] Lane, [*An Arabic–English Lexicon*], vol. I, [(London, 1863–93)], [p.] 268*c*, after the Qāmūs and Tāj el-'Arūs'.

96. *HPAP*, p. 257.

97. Lane, I, p. 268*a sub* ابهم.

98. Cf. أَبْهَمُ which the Qamus instances as a rock 'having no fissures in it' (Lane, I, p. 269*b sub* مُبْهَمَةٌ).

99. R. L. Cleveland, 'The Excavation of the Conway High Place (Petra) and Soundings at Khirbet Adr', *AASOR* XXXIV–XXXV (1960), p. 78. Albright assigned to Cleveland the task of writing this, the official report of the excavation.

100. Albright's suggestion that the strange expressions of 1 K xii 31 and 2 K xvii 29, 32 (variously *bêṯ bāmôṯ* and *bêṯ habbāmôṯ*) may mean 'house of stelae', though attractive, must be dismissed. Long ago *GK* (§124*r*)

showed how they are allowable alternatives to *bāttê habbāmôṯ*, 'shrines of the bamoth', which is the phrase in 1 K xiii 32 and 2 K xxiii 19 (cf. *bêṯ 'āḇôṯ* as the plural of *bêṯ 'āḇ* in Ex vi 14 and Nb i 2, 4ff etc.). This is not to deny that shrine buildings with stelae in them did not exist (such as the small one found at Hazor, Area C). It is merely to affirm that these stelae were not termed *bāmôṯ*.

Albright also finds support for his theory from the fact that the LXX in the Pentateuch 'regularly rendered *bâmāh* by *stēlē*' (*HPAP*, p. 248). In point of fact this only happens in four places (Lv xxvi 30; Nb xxi 28, xxii 41, xxxiii 52). But whether this translation provides any reliable evidence on the meaning of *bāmôṯ* is open to question on at least three accounts: the possibility of a variant Hebrew text behind the LXX rendering cannot be ruled out (? *maṣṣēḇôṯ*, since στήλη so regularly represents this word); the LXX translators continuously had great difficulty in understanding the word *bāmâ*, as many other instances show (see discussion of this in Chapter II); most important, however, is the fact that στήλη is *not* the word used in the five passages of Kings under discussion.

101. Cf. 1 K xiv 23, where there are listed side by side: *bāmôṯ ûmaṣṣēḇôṯ wa'ᵃšērîm*, clearly referring to three separate objects.

102. While there is no question that Hebrew *bōhen* is directly related to Arabic *'ibhām* 'thumb', the latter has nothing to do with either stone stelae or mountain peaks, but rather is derived from √بهم IV meaning 'shut, closed'. Tāj el-'Arūs notes that one says of the thumb تُبْهِمُ الكَفَّ meaning 'It closes upon (the palm of) the hand' (Lane, I p. 268*a*, *b*). The derivation of *bōhen* will therefore be parallel.

NOTES TO CHAPTER II (pp. 29–36)

1. 1 S ix 12–25.
2. 1 S x 5, 13. The very name of the place suggests that it is a hill.
3. 1 K xi 7.
4. This is not specifically stated, but it is the most natural interpretation of 2 K xxiii 16 where 'the tombs there on the mount' are in the immediate vicinity of the bamah.
5. E.g. 2 K xvi 4, xvii 9–10; Ezk xx 28, etc. See W. L. Holladay, 'On Every High Hill . . .', *VT* XI (1961), pp. 170–6, for an interesting attempt to trace the development of this phrase through its sixteen occurrences in the Old Testament.
6. 1 K xiii 32; 2 K xvii 9, 29, xxiii 5.
7. 2 K xxiii 8 (cf. discussion of the text of this verse in Chapter I, note 41). This bamah seems to have been positioned directly outside the governor's residence. Was it a private bamah for his personal use? – similar to the little shrine found in the street outside a palatial building at Hazor (see *BA* XXII (1959), p. 14).
8. Following *BH*[3] suggested emendation.
9. See further discussion of this verse on pp. 53 and 76 nn. 63–5.
10. Jr xxxii 35; cf. vii 31.
11. 2 K xxiii 8, 15; 2 Ch xxxi 1, xxxiii 3.
12. Dt xii 2; 2 K xxi 3; Ezk vi 3.
13. 2 K xviii 4, xviii 22 (= Is xxxvi 7), xxiii 19; 2 Ch xxx 14, etc.

14. 1 K xxii 43 (44 in MT); 2 K xii 3 (4 in MT), xiv 4, xv 4, 35, xvi 4, xvii 11, xxiii 5; 2 Ch xxviii 4, 25 all specifically state that incense was burned on bamoth.
15. 1 S ix 19.
16. Is xvi 12.
17. Ezk xvi 16ff.
18. Jr vii 31, xix 5, xxxii 35; Ezk xvi 20. There are of course other references to child sacrifices, but these four are specific about the close relation of this form of sacrifice to bamoth.
19. 1 K xxii 43 (44 in MT); 2 K xii 3 (4 in MT), xiv 4, xv 4, 35. Similar descriptions of sacrifice and/or incense-burning *babbāmôṯ* occur in 1 K iii 2; 2 K xvi 4, xvii 11; and 2 Ch xxviii 4, 25, xxxiii 17.
20. 1 K xiv 23 *et passim.*
21. 2 K xxi 3 does not discount this assertion. The altars are specifically stated to have been erected in the Jerusalem Temple (verse 4), while the bamoth will have been scattered around the Judean countryside. The same applies in xviii 22, where Hezekiah is said to have removed 'bamoth and altars', commanding both 'Judah and Jerusalem' to worship at the central altar. There would seem to be a careful parallelism here: the Judahites are to forsake their bamoth, but the Jerusalemites the additional altars in the Temple (cf. xvi 10ff.).
22. For instance, J. A. Montgomery, *The Book of Kings* (*ICC*, Edinburgh, 1951), p. 534, 'Omission of the long bracketed section [all but the first four and last four words of the verse] is necessary to reduce a most conflate passage'; or J. Gray, *I & II Kings* (London, 1964), p. 671 'This ill-constructed sentence is suspect.'
23. Following the Hebrew text reflected in LXX^{BL}, which appears to have omitted *wᵉ'eṯ*.
24. *√nṯṣ* is a perfectly satisfactory verb to be used of the bamah as much as of the altar: cf. its use with *bāmâ* as object in verse 8. It must have been ignorance of the real nature of bamoth which allowed Montgomery (*Book of Kings*) to make the inaccurate comment, 'an altar can be destroyed, but hardly a high-place'.
25. Following the LXX, since the burning of a (stone) bamah and altar seems so unlikely an event.
26. This is how the Syriac Peshitta understood it.
27. Only the Books of Kings have been considered above, because they are prose. These findings may well be applicable also in the prophetic books; but this is not demonstrable on account of their poetic parallelisms. It is never possible to be sure whether a parallelism is synonymous or synthetical. For instance, in Ho x 8 it is impossible to say whether or not 'the bamoth of Aven' are regarded as the same objects as the parallel 'their altars' in the next line.
28. This Greek understanding of *bāmâ* is significant in that it correctly retains the idea of 'mountain height', which a bamah was meant to represent (the same Greek word is frequently used to represent *mārôm*, a non-cultic 'height'). That the LXX translators by and large had an accurate idea of what a bamah was is shown by three other translations: ὕψος 'height' (2 S i 19, 25, xxii 34; Am iv 13; Mi i 3); βουνός 'hill, mound' (1 S x 13; Ps lxxvii (lxxviii) 58); and more significantly βαμα (1 S ix 12, 13, 14, 19, 25, x 5, (?) xi 8; 1 Ch xvi 39, xxi 29; 2 Ch i 13). The latter transliteration shows that at least in some places the translators were aware that *bāmâ* was a technical term, and as such was best left untranslated. On the general reliability of the LXX as preserving accurate details of the pre-exilic cult, see S. Daniel, *Recherches sur le Vocabulair du Culte dans la Septante* (Paris, 1966).

It is clear, however, that the meaning of the archaic form *bāmᵒṯê* was lost by the time that the LXX was translated, and such wildly divergent paraphrases as ἰσχύς (Dt xxxii 13), τραχήλος (Dt xxxiii 29), ἐπάνω (Is xiv 14), ἀγαθός (Is lviii 14), ἐδάφος (Jb ix 8) were used.

See also the concordance appendixed to this monograph.

29. All occurrences are in the Prophets: Ho x 8; Am vii 9; Is xv 2, xvi 12; Jr vii 31 (?32), (?)xxx 18 (xlix 2), xxxi (xlviii) 35, xxxix (xxxii) 35. Symmachus also uses βωμός in Jr xix 5. A unique LXX rendering of *bāmôṯ* is found in 2 Ch xiv 4(5): θυσιαστήρια. It would be convenient to use this as yet another evidence that bamoth were regarded as altars. But in view of the fact that in verse 2 the usual rendering τὰ ὑψηλὰ is found, θυσιαστήρια may not be a rendering of *bâmôṯ* at all, but merely a copyist's careless repetition of a word used two verses earlier.

30. Apart from the two meanings discussed here, the other meanings given are: 'a tomb, cairn' (late and once only); the title of a poem; 'an altar-shaped cake'; the name of a (?) Syrian god Ζεὺς Βωμός; and two other unrelated occurrences.

31. There exists an interesting example of βωμός as a loan-word in a Semitic context clearly meaning 'pedestal (for a statue)'. A Nabatean inscription (*Répertoire d'Epigraphie Sémitique* IV (Paris, 1919), pp. 55ff, inscription no. 2117) on the side of a small block of stone (42 cm. long and 33 cm. high), designed as the base for a statue, reads:

'In the year . . . there was made by . . . this pedestal for the statue of Galis (בומס צלם גלשו) . . .'

The original publisher of this inscription translated בומס צלם as 'altar of the statue'. But the references in *LSJ* suggest that בומס here has no cultic connotation at all, and is used in the straightforward sense of 'pedestal'. The fact that the pedestal in this case also looked like an altar is beside the point – in the nature of things, every pedestal would have looked like an altar, and the word βωμός could describe either object, since the primary concept contained in the word is geometric, not cultic.

32. See Supplement to *LSJ* (Oxford, 1968).

33. In *ARI*, p. 202, note 24, Albright notes the possible Phoenician derivation of Greek βωμός: 'In favor of it is not only the almost identical cultic meaning of the two words, but also their etymological form.' By contrast, in *HPAP*, pp. 248f., he supposes that the cultic use of bamoth arose in the first place as a result of religious rites at stone cairns or tumuli such as those raised over graves at Serābîṭ el-khâdim (in Sinai). But the meaning of βωμός (see note 34 below) militates against this supposition.

34. W. K. C. Guthrie, *The Greeks and Their Gods* (London, 1950), pp. 221f., shows the great contrast that existed in Greek religion between worship of the Olympian gods and of the chthonic spirits. Not only are details of the rites appropriate for each totally different (methods of slaughtering sacrifices, choice of victims, type of shrine, time of day, gestures for prayer all differed), but the actual language describing these rites differed. Thus the verb 'to sacrifice' to the Olympians is θύειν, but to the *chthonoi* is ἐναγίζειν. This differentiation is related to the type of hearth used: that for the *chthonoi* was at ground level (so that the blood could drain directly into the soil) and is called ἐσχάρα; that for the Olympians was a raised structure and is termed βωμός. This Greek usage is further (indirect) evidence against Albright's theory that bamoth were associated with a cult of the dead.

35. For instance Herodotus VI. 108: while offerings were being presented, ἱκέται ἱζόμενοι ἐπὶ τὸν βωμὸν.
36. Herodotus II. 125: ἐποιήθη δε ὧδε αὕτη ἡ πυραμίς, ἀναβαθμῶν τρόπον, τὰς μετεξέτεροι κρόσσας, οἱ δὲ βωμίδας ὀνομάζουσι.
37. A third word which might also appear to be an exception is βωμολογεύομαι 'to play the buffoon'. But it too is related to βωμός through the cult, referring to the riotous or drunken behaviour associated with temple feasts before the altar.
38. Ex xxxiv 13; Nb xxiii 1, 2, 4, 14, 29, 30; Dt vii 5, xii 3; Jos xxii 10, 11, 16, 19, 23, 26, 34; 2 Ch xxxi 1; Is xvii 8, xxvii 9; Jr xi 13.
39. The use of βωμός for the altars built by Balak (Nb xxiii) and the trans-Jordan tribes (Jos xxii) is interesting. The theological presuppositions of the LXX translators must have compelled them to regard these altars as unorthodox, and so they employed the derogatory word βωμός with its pagan implications. There is one instance in the LXX where βωμός is used of a Yahweh altar: Nb iii 10. But significantly, this is a passage which is a LXX addition to the MT; the presence of this word here probably indicates that the LXX addition is late (see below and note 41). Daniel (*Recherches*) has examined in detail the LXX translations of *mizbēaḥ*, and points out how in the Pentateuch, Isaiah and Jeremiah a strict *theological* distinction is preserved between βωμός and θυσιαστήριον.
40. θυσιαστήριον is always used of the altar of burnt-offering in the Temple (i 21, 54, 59, iv *passim*, v 1, vi 7, vii 36), while βωμός is always used of the altars set up by the Hellenizers. An outstanding example of the scrupulous distinction between the two words comes in i 59, 'They offered sacrifice on the altar which was upon the altar of burnt-offering: θυσιάζοντες ἐπὶ τὸν βωμόν ὃς ἦν ἐπὶ τοῦ θυσιαστηρίου.'
41. βωμός is so used in 2 M xiii 8; Si l 12, 14 (where θυσιαστήριον is used in the same context – verse 15); *Antiquities* ix 163, 165, 223, 263, x 53, xi 308 (where θυσιαστήριον is also used in the same context). But while βωμός can be used interchangeably with θυσιαστήριον for the Temple altar, the reverse is not the case. θυσιαστήριον is never used of pagan altars. In other words, at all times βωμός retained its character as the natural word to use for pagan altars.
42. Nb xxi 19, 20, 28, xxii 41, and Jos xiii 17. These may be compared with the place-name *bmt* in line 27 of the Mesha Inscription.
43. Is xv 2, xvi 12, and Jr xlviii 35.
44. 1 K xi 7.

NOTES TO CHAPTER III (pp. 37–54)

1. Cf. C. C. McCowan's pungent and sometimes derisive remarks about attempts to identify 'cult objects' and 'cult sites' at Megiddo in 'Hebrew High Places and Cult Remains', *JBL* LXIX (1950), pp. 205–19.
2. A recent example is R. G. Boling, *BA* XXXII 4 (1969), p. 101, who considers that the rock outcrop at Tananir corresponds to the man-made bamah at Nahariya. Similarly, J. L. Kelso, in discussing a great rock surface used as an altar at Bethel in Chalcolithic times, uses the expression 'open air sacrificial shrine' interchangeably with 'high place' – e.g. 'This bare mountain-top was the ancient high place . . . where the Canaanites worshipped El' (J. L. Kelso, 'The Excavation of Bethel (1934–1960)', *AASOR* XXXIX (1968), p. 21).

Rather than prejudice the discussion of the use of such rock altars by using terminology commonly applied to later built structures, it would be more satisfactory to use straightforward descriptive nomenclature, and call them 'rock altars'.

3. G. Horsfield and A. Conway, 'Historical and Topographical Notes on Edom, with an account of the first excavations at Petra', *Geographical Journal* LXXVI (1930), 5, pp. 369–88.
4. Albright produced a preliminary report of the 1934 excavations in 'The Excavation of the Conway High Place at Petra', *BASOR* LVII (1935), pp. 18–26; but a full report did not appear till twenty-five years later.
5. Cleveland, 'The Conway High Place'.
6. *Ibid*, p. 78.
7. Cleveland entitles the section (pp. 75–8) 'The High Place in the Ancient Semitic World', but in fact it is simply a discussion of rocks and rites associated with them. He cites five examples of circular processional ways. Only two of them come from the pre-Islamic period. They were found at Nejrân (on the border between Saudi Arabia and the Yemen) and at Ḍhofâr (on the Indian Ocean Coast). The latter site was used from the second century B.C. to the fourth century A.D. Both these examples are too remote in distance, time and culture to have any bearing whatever on Israelite bamoth. The other three examples cited are from the Islamic period – namely the Dome of the Rock at Jerusalem, the Ka'ba at Mecca, and the tomb of the third Imâm at Kerbelā – and therefore are even less likely to reflect anything of Old Testament Israelite rites. All in all, this adds up to a negligible amount of evidence in favour of ceremonial processional ways around rocks in the Old Testament period.
8. P. J. Parr, 'Le "Conway High Place" à Pétra: une nouvelle interprétation', *RB* LXIX (1962), pp. 64–79.
9. *Ibid*, p. 65. The English translation here and below is mine.
10. Horsfield had already discovered the foundation trench of one of these walls, and had associated the Conway 'High Place' with the town's defences – though only at a late stage in its history (G. and A. Horsfield, 'Sela–Petra, the Rock, of Edom and Nabatene', *QDAP* VII (1938), p. 7). Albright and Cleveland disregarded this. But Parr's discovery of the second wall on the other side of the tower now make the defensive interpretation of the structure inevitable.
11. Parr, 'Le "Conway High Place"', p. 71.
12. See his description of the cultic use of the site in *HPAP*, pp. 256f.
13. Parr, 'Le "Conway High Place"', p. 72.
14. *Ibid*, p. 76. Parr accepts that they are 'undoubtedly of a votive nature, but without what that might imply – any connection of the monument itself with the cult, as Albright supposes'.
15. *Ibid*, p. 76. Italics mine.
16. Cleveland, 'The Conway High Place', p. 78. Albright has briefly expressed his disagreement with Parr's findings in a book review (*Bibliotheca Orientalis* XXI (1964), p. 67). He accuses Parr of 'so many mistakes . . . a palpably absurd explanation of an original tower in a Roman city wall', and promises a 'prolonged rebuttal' elsewhere. This rebuttal has never appeared.
17. M. Dothan, 'Excavations at Nahariya', *IEJ* VI (1956), pp. 14–25.
18. *Ibid*, p. 14.
19. Dothan considers that 'it does not seem likely that the temple complex

stood isolated and at a great distance from a settlement. The settlement must be sought in the tell on the south bank of the River Ga'aton, which is 900 m. distant from the temple' (*ibid*, p. 24).

20. *Ibid*, p. 17.
21. The aerial photograph Plate 1*c* gives a good impression of its circular shape.
22. Italics mine. C. Epstein also stresses the natural eminence of the bamah's position: in EB III it 'already occupied a dominant position above surrounding buildings. From this time onwards the sacred area continued to be higher than the associated buildings around it' ('An Interpretation of the Megiddo Sacred Area During Middle Bronze II', *IEJ* xv (1965), p. 205).
23. G. Loud, *Megiddo II* (Chicago, 1948), p. 73. A good idea of the shape of the bamah may be gained from the two photographs, figs. 164 and 165, which also show the ascent stairs. Fig. 166 is a close-up photograph of the surrounding debris with an ox(?)-jaw clearly showing.
24. *Ibid*, p. 76. Loud's stratigraphy and dating of the Megiddo bamah has lately been much debated – see K. M. Kenyon, 'Some Notes on the Early and Middle Bronze Age Strata of Megiddo', *Eretz-Israel* v, and more recently C. Epstein, 'An Interpretation', for discussion of the various problems involved. But whatever the exact date of the bamah may be, Loud's description of its physical appearance still stands.
25. The quotation is my own translation from the preliminary report submitted by B. Mazar (the excavator) in *RB* LXX (1963), p. 576. A detailed report was published in *BIES* XXVII in Hebrew, but was not available to me.
26. D. Ussishkin, 'The "Ghassulian" Temple in Ein Gedi and the Origin of the Hoard from Nahal Mishmar', *BA* XXXIV (1971), p. 31. Fig. 17 clearly shows a low conical platform, apparently built of rough stones.
27. Y. Aharoni, 'Arad: its Inscriptions and Temple', *BA* XXXI (1968), p. 19.
28. The shape is a very curious and unnatural one. Several questions present themselves: Was it originally designed this way, or is it a partially destroyed circular bamah? What is its relation to the altar – is it contemporary or a later addition? Are the burnt bones to be related to the altar or the bamah? Answers to these questions will have to await publication of the full excavation report.
29. Aharoni, 'Arad', p. 8. A photograph of the seal and its impression is given in fig. 6, and clearly shows a conical structure surrounded by four walls.
30. Cf. the setting of the bamoth at Megiddo, En-Gedi and Arad (Stratum XII).
31. R. Amiram, 'Tumuli West of Jerusalem', *IEJ* VIII (1958), pp. 205–27. Pottery dates the use of the sites within the narrow range 'second half of eighth and the seventh century BC' (p. 222).
32. *Ibid*, p. 207.
33. *Ibid*, p. 205.
34. *Ibid*, p. 211.
35. *Ibid*, p. 215.
36. *Ibid*, p. 216.
37. Amiram originally was prepared 'to interpret the whole site as a high place (*bamah*)', chiefly influenced by the lack of any 'interment or any trace of human bones in the pit or beside it, and the ceremonial character of the flight of steps leading to the platform' (pp. 226f.). But following the publication of *HPAP*, she found herself pursuaded by Albright's theory

that 'the *bamah* served two purposes at one and the same time: that of a burial and that of a cult place'. Albright (*HPAP*, p. 250) convinced that bamoth were burial cairns, identifies these tumuli as such, although being forced to admit 'there may not have been any burials inside or under them'. They were 'apparently commemorative rather then funerary'. He continues his speculation: 'In fact, it is perfectly possible that the tumuli . . . were erected to commemorate deceased heroes whose graves had long been forgotten or who were not mortal at all!' (!)

38. Y. Yadin, *Hazor II* (Jerusalem, 1960), pp. 130ff., where the 'Cult Place', locus 8019, is discussed.
39. *Ibid*, p. 132. It should, however, be noted that one of the excavators, I. Dunayevsky, was unconvinced about this cultic interpretation of the evidence. In a lengthy footnote (p. 130) he points out that 'Locus 8019 was not completely cleared'.
40. *Ibid*, p. 130. A good photograph of the structure appears in Plate XL; larger stones marking the curb edge can be clearly seen.
41. 'A big platform made of small rough stones . . . which served most probably as a cultic high-place or bamah', 'Further Light on Biblical Hazor', *BA* XX (1957), p. 45.
42. Y. Yadin *et al.*, *Hazor III–IV* (Jerusalem, 1961), Area H, locus 2554, described as 'Cult Place' in captions to Plates CXI² and CXII¹.
43. Y. Yadin, 'Excavations at Hazor, 1958', *IEJ* IX (1959), p. 83.
44. *RB* LXXIV (1967), p. 71. Translation mine.
45. *RB* LXXI (1964), p. 396; *RB* LXXII (1965), pp. 558f.; *BA* XXXI (1968), pp. 18ff.
46. Aharoni, 'Arad', p. 19. See also the accompanying photograph, fig. 13.
47. A. Biran, *IEJ* XX (1970), p. 118. A good impression of the monumental flight of steps be gained from Plate 2(b) in this monograph.
48. G. E. Wright, *Shechem: the Biography of a Biblical City* (London, 1965), pp. 110–12, describes how 'Structure 968' was found at the lowest level underneath a succession of temples. 'What its function was, we do not know, except that it is something extensive made by human effort. It is a kind of platform, *ca.* 1 m high, the outer sides of which are faced with stone, while the interior is made of packed earth and stones topped by a layer of fine yellow (marly) earth.' Pottery jars had fallen off the top of it and were found in pieces down the sloping sides of the structure. 'I thought immediately of a large earthen altar at Megiddo, its top and sides lined with stone . . . and its date in the same period as our structure. On the other hand, we cannot rule out the possibility that it is an earthen wall.'

   Because of its location underneath so many other structures, it was not possible to excavate it completely. Decisive conclusions as to its nature cannot therefore be reached. But in view of its position underneath the later temples, it is tempting to give it a cultic interpretation: as being the earliest bamah which marks the site of the first Shechemites' shrine. Regarding its relation to the city, Wright says 'it is clear that a major construction job was done . . . first to level [the site] and then to build on it. All this was done before the earliest-known city fortification at Shechem . . . was built. The structures described above were evidently outside the main confines of the city before *ca.* 1750 B.C. Yet work here was so extensive *ca.* 1800 B.C. that we must conclude that for whatever purpose the area was used, it was deemed very important.'

As noted by Wright, its resemblance to the Megiddo bamah is striking, but with one notable exception – it was a straight-sided structure, whereas that at Megiddo is circular. It is best classified with the second type of rectangular bamah.

But because of incomplete data, we must resist the temptation to use Structure 968 at Shechem as an example of a bamah – although it may well be one. It must remain anonymous as a 'large earthen platform with stones fixed along its outer edge to prevent erosion . . . erected for a purpose about which we dare not speculate at this time. Yet its size suggests a public function of considerable importance' (p. 121).

The results of further excavation in 1965 (*BASOR* 180, pp. 26f.) do not materially either add or detract from the above inconclusive remarks.

49. Wright, *Shechem*, fig. 50. This photograph clearly shows the white marly bricks over the mud bricks, which in turn rest on the plastered floor of the preceding Temple 1[a].
50. *Ibid*, p. 93.
51. *Ibid*, pp. 233f.
52. It is tempting to ask whether the Hazor locus 8019 may not also have been used in the same manner. For just as at Shechem (and Arad Stratum x – see below), when the altar was destroyed, its platform was left, so the Hazor platform may originally have had an altar on it. The huge 5-ton monolith altar found in the same Square could possibly be this very altar, for it was found resting at an unnatural angle – apparently its huge size defeated its destructors.
53. G. E. Wright, *Biblical Archaeology*[2] (London, 1962), fig. 175, illustrates the difference in floor level clearly. It is, of course, true that this rock-cut method of construction is unique to Petra and comparatively late in date (probably first century B.C.). But it is quite clear that the makers of this sanctuary were at pains to copy a pattern of things already established in traditional *built* sanctuaries. For instance, the free standing obelisks nearby witness to the retention of ideas surrounding ancient Canaanite *maṣṣēḇōṯ* (cf. W. F. Albright, *Archaeology of Palestine* (London, 1960), pp. 163f.).
54. *RB* LXXII (1965), p. 559, and Plate XXIX*a*; 'Arad', pp. 18–23, and fig. 14.
55. *RB* LXXII (1965), p. 559. Translation mine.
56. 'Arad', p. 23.
57. Cf. the offerings similarly placed on the Hazor bamah (locus 8019).
58. So Albright: 'I see no reason to doubt that this passage refers to the original altar of burnt offering as built by Solomon, presumably described from memory' (*ARI*, p. 217, note 81). If the whole passage about the altar measurements is an insertion of a self-contained unit (as many commentators suppose), then the likelihood of the preservation of an early temple tradition is increased.
59. Indeed A. Parrot, *The Temple of Jerusalem* (London, 1957), p. 63, comments: 'This characteristic design so closely resembles the relief in the Louvre which shows a ziggurat ornamented with horns that *it would be difficult to deny the relationship between the altar of Ezekiel's vision and the Mesopotamian ziggurat.*' Italics mine.
60. For instance Cooke is declaredly influenced by the meaning of *ḥêq* in 1 K xxii 35 – 'The hollow interior of a chariot' – and so 'the general description . . . suggests a platform or base, into which the square above appeared to sink, as into a bosom' (*Ezekiel*, p. 467). The situation is further complicated by the uncertain senses of *g*ᵉ*ḇûlāh* and *ś*ᵉ*p̄āṯāh* in the verse. Thus some

consider that the top of the *ḥêq* was at the same level as the surrounding ground, but separated from it by a channel and a low wall (to stop people falling into the channel). Others visualise a *ḥêq* raised above ground level, but having a low wall at its outer edge, thus creating a channel between the wall and the lowest cube of the altar. In either case it is assumed that the function of the channel was to catch the blood from the altar. But this is nowhere stated in the text, and hardly seems necessary for Ezekiel's theology, since the whole temple mount was already separated from the rest of the profane land. But while details about the shape of the base remain unclear, there is no doubt that *ḥêq* was the name of the base.

61. *hr'l*; cf. Akkadian *arallu*. See Albright, *ARI*, p. 151, and also his discussion of the meaning of these Akkadian terms in *JBL* XXXIX (1920), pp. 137–42.

62. An early exception is C. F. Keil, who is quite prepared to accept the integrity of MT *gab*: 'the חֵיק with its moulding is designated גַּב the back or support of the altar, and is thereby distinguished from the altar itself' (*Commentary on the Prophecies of Ezekiel* (Edinburgh, 1876), vol. II, p. 287). More recently W. Zimmerli, *Ezechiel* (Neukirchen, 1955–69), pp. 1089f., accepts *gab* as meaning *Sockel des Altars*. K. Galling also took *gab* as the name of the lowest section of the altar: A. Bertholet, *Hezekiel* (Tübingen, 1936), p. 153 (Beitrag von K. Galling). But in the new edition of the same series by G. Fohrer (1955), he takes the view that the word should be read as 'height' with the LXX (pp. 238ff.).

63. In Ezk xvi 24, 31, 39, *gab* is variously represented by ὄικημα πορνικόν (verse 24) and τὸ πορνεῖον (verses 31 and 39). No doubt these expressions reflect what happened at a *gab*, but they can only be regarded as temporisations, not translations.

64. *BH*[3] implies that *rmh* is a transcriptional error for *bmh*. This would be very convenient for our present thesis, but there is absolutely no evidence for this in the Versions, either here or in verses 31 or 39. It is true that confusion over precisely these two words does occur in 1 S xxii 6, where *rmh* of MT is transliterated in LXX^{A} as ραμμα and in LXX^{BL} as βαμα. This probably indicates that two recensions of the Hebrew text existed contemporaneously. However, *BH*[3] is probably wrong in inferring that the same thing has happened in Ezk xvi 24: for the same pair of words (*gab* and *rāmâ*) also occur in verses 31 and 39, and it is unlikely that the same corruption has happened in three separate places.

65. The precise meaning of *gab* is difficult to determine. It has no verbal root in Hebrew, and occurs in a wide variety of contexts, suggesting the meanings: human *back* (Ps cxxix 3), *boss* of a shield (Jb xv 26), *earth-works* (Jb xiii 12), *eye-brows* (Lv xiv 9), *rim* of a wheel (1 K vii 33), and most significantly of some man-built structure in connection with the cult (Ezk xvi 24, 31, 39). Here the RSV translation of *gab* by 'vaulted chamber' is unsuitable. *gab* is a direct parallel in the verse to *rāmâ* 'a raised place', and will mean a 'raised platform' built up of loose stones such as archaeology has laid bare in certain sites (cf. *KB*[3] *ad loc. Wülste d. Altarsockels*). This conclusion is confirmed by the associated verb *wattiḇnî*: for √*bnh* is the verb used everywhere to describe the construction of bamoth. While in verse 39, when the *rāmâ* (the synonymn of *gab*) is destroyed, √*ntṣ* is the verb used; elsewhere this same verb is used in relation to the destruction of bamoth.

66. Herodotus's choice of βωμίς in describing the pyramids is particularly significant, for the pyramids have a formation identical with Ezekiel's tiered altar and our Type II bamah – a square structure built on a plinth which projects on all sides.

SELECT BIBLIOGRAPHY

Y. Aharoni, 'Arad: its Inscriptions and Temple', *BA* XXXI (1968), pp. 2–32.

'The Israelite Sanctuary at Arad' in D. N. Freedman and J. C. Greenfield (eds.), *New Directions in Biblical Archaeology* (New York, 1969), pp. 25–39.

brief excavation reports in *RB* LXXI (1964), p. 396; LXXII (1965), pp. 558ff.; and LXXIV (1967), pp. 69ff. [on Tell Arad].

W. F. Albright, *Archaeology of Palestine* (London, 1960).

Archaeology and the Religion of Israel[4] (Baltimore, 1956).

'The High Place in Ancient Palestine' in *Volume du Congrès, Strasbourg* (Supplements to *VT* IV) (Leiden, 1957), pp. 242–58.

JBL LVII (1938), p. 227 [on Jb ix 8].

'The Excavation of the Conway High Place at Petra', *BASOR* LVII (1935), pp. 18–26.

R. Amiram, 'Tumuli West of Jerusalem', *IEJ* VIII (1958), pp. 205–27.

D. R. Ap-Thomas, 'Two Notes on Isaiah' in E. C. B. MacLaurin (ed.), *Essays in Honour of Griffithes Wheeler Thatcher 1863–1950* (Sydney, 1967), pp. 45–61 [on Is ii 22].

A. Biran, brief excavation report in *IEJ* XX (1970), p. 118 [on Tel Dan].

R. L. Cleveland, 'The Excavation of the Conway High Place (Petra) and Soundings at Khirbet Adr', *AASOR* XXXIV–XXXV (1960), pp. 55–78.

F. M. Cross and D. N. Freedman, 'The Blessing of Moses', *JBL* LXVII (1948), pp. 191–210 [on Dt XXXIII 29].

M. Dahood, 'Hebrew–Ugaritic Lexicography – I', *Biblica* XLIV (1963), p. 302 (*bmh*).

'Hebrew–Ugaritic Lexicography – II', *Biblica* XLV (1964), p. 398 (*g'wh*).

Psalms I (Garden City, 1966), p. 115 [on *bāmᵉṯê*].

S. Daniel, *Recherches sur le Vocabulaire du Culte dans la Septante* (Paris, 1966).

M. Dothan, 'Excavations at Nahariya', *IEJ* VI (1956), pp. 14–25.

G. R. Driver, 'Isaiah I–XXXIX: Textual and Linguistic Problems', *JSS* XIII (1968), p. 38 [on Is vi 13).

C. Epstein, 'An Interpretation of the Megiddo Sacred Area During Middle Bronze II', *IEJ* XV (1965), pp. 204–21.

A. Guillaume, 'A Contribution to Hebrew Lexicography', *BSOAS* XVI (1954), p. 10 [on Is liii9].

W. K. C. Guthrie, *The Greeks and their Gods* (London, 1950), pp. 221f. [on βωμός/ἐσχάρα].

M. Held, 'Studies in Comparative Semitic Lexicography', in H. G. Güterbock and T. Jacobsen (eds.), *Studies in Honor of Benno Landsberger* (Chicago, 1965), pp. 402ff.

D. R. Hillers, *Treaty Curses and the Old Testament Prophets* (Rome, 1964), pp. 53f. [on Mi iii 12 = Jr xxvi 18].

W. L. Holladay, 'On Every High Hill . . .', *VT* XI (1964), pp. 170–6.

G. Horsfield and A. Conway, 'Historical and Topographical Notes on Edom, with an account of the first excavations at Petra', *Geographical Journal* LXXVI (1930), pp. 369–88.

G. and A. Horsfield, 'Sela–Petra, the Rock, of Edom and Nabatene', *QDAP* VII (1938), pp. 1–42.

S. Iwry, 'MAṢṢĒBĀH and BĀMĀH in 1Q Isaiah^A 6[13]', *JBL* LXXVI (1957), pp. 225–32.

J. L. Kelso *et al.*, 'The Excavation of Bethel (1934–1960)', *AASOR* XXXIX (1968), pp. 20f.

B. A. Levine, 'Cult Places, Israelite', *Encyclopaedia Judaica* (Jerusalem, 1971), pp. 1162–9.

G. Loud, *Megiddo II* (Chicago, 1948), pp. 73ff.

B. Mazar, brief excavation report in *RB* LXX (1963), pp. 575–7 [on En-Gedi].

C. C. McCowan, 'Hebrew High Places and Cult Remains', *JBL* LXIX (1950), pp. 205–19.

D. Neiman, '*PGR*: a Canaanite Cult-Object in the Old Testament', *JBL* LXVII (1948), pp. 55–60.

P. J. Parr, 'Le "Conway High Place" à Pétra: une nouvelle interprétation', *RB* LXIX (1962), pp. 64–79.

J. Sawyer, 'The Qumran Reading of Isaiah 6, 13', *Annual of the Swedish Theological Institute* III (1964), pp. 111–13 [on Is vi 13].

A. Sperber, *A Historical Grammar of Biblical Hebrew* (Leiden, 1966), p. 40 [on *bām^eṯê*].

H. Torczyner, *Bulletin of the Jewish Palestine Exploration Society* III (1933), pp. 9–18.

D. Ussishkin, 'The "Ghassulian" Temple in Ein Gedi and the Origin of the Hoard from Nahal Mishmar', *BA* xxxiv (1971), pp. 23–39.

R. de Vaux, *Ancient Israel* (London, 1961), pp. 56–61, 284–8, 331–44, 406–14, and 433–46.

L. H. Vincent, 'La Notion Biblique du Haut-Lieu', *RB* LV (1948), pp. 245–78 and 438–45.

D. Winton Thomas, 'A Consideration of Isaiah LIII in the Light of Recent Textual and Philological Studies', in H. Cazelles (ed.), *De Mari à Qumrân* (Gembloux, 1969).

G. E. Wright, *Shechem: the Biography of a Biblical City* (London, 1965), pp. 80–122 and 229–34.

Y. Yadin, *Hazor II* (Jerusalem, 1960), pp. 130ff.

'Further Light on Biblical Hazor', *BA* xx (1957), pp. 34–47.

'Excavations at Hazor, 1958', *IEJ* IX (1959), pp. 74–88.

INDEX OF BIBLICAL REFERENCES

INDEX OF SEMITIC WORDS

INDEX OF AUTHORS CITED IN SELECT BIBLIOGRAPHY

GENERAL INDEX

altar 31ff., 35, 37, 39, 41, 42, 46, 48f., 50, 51ff., 55

Baal texts 4ff., 10f.
bāmâ
  cognates in Akkadian 6ff., 10ff., 23ff., 25; Arabic 26ff.; Greek, 22, 23, 25, 26, 34f., 53; Moabite 3, 15, 25, 36; Ugaritic 4ff., 10ff., 23ff., 25
  derivation 3, 21f.
  LXX translations 3, 20, 33ff.
bamah
  construction 30f., 38
  geographical distribution 36
  location 29f.
  rites performed at 31ff.
  use by archaeologists 37, 39, 40, 41, 42f., 46, 47, 48
burial, manner of 17f.

cairn 26, 34
Conway High Place 26, 28, 37ff.
cult of the dead 1, 16, 18, 27f., 55

Dead Sea scrolls 16, 22

En-Gedi 41f.

Hazor 46

incense 31

Megiddo 41
Mesha Inscription 3, 36
Moabite 3, 15, 25, 36
mythology 9, 11f., 24, 25, 55

Nahariya 40f.

Petra
  Conway High Place 26, 28, 37ff.
  Robinson High Place 49
platforms 12, 13, 29, 31, 32, 34f., 44 45, 46, 47, 48f., 51, 52ff., 55
prayer 31
prostitution 31

sacrifice 31f., 34, 41, 44
Shechem 48f.
stele 19, 26, 28

Tell Arad 42f., 47, 50
Tel Dan 47f.
tumuli near Jerusalem 43f.

water cult 42

Yahweh myth 9, 11f., 24, 25, 55

CONCORDANCE

of the occurrences of במה together with the LXX translations in each case

The following concordance contains every occurrence of *bāmâ* in the Massoretic Text and the equivalents in the Septuagint. The edition of the MT used is R. Kittel (ed.), *Biblia Hebraica*[7] (Stuttgart, 1951). That of the LXX is A. Rahlfs (ed.), *Septuaginta*[6] (Stuttgart, n.d.).

Numerous variants in the manuscripts of the LXX, of course, exist. But none of these seems significant for our purposes, most being inner-Greek variants of the kind found in 2 Chronicles i 13, where B has μαβα for βαμα.

A further problem exists in attempting to relate the Greek text to the Hebrew, because the LXX translators may have used a Hebrew text different from that of the Massoretes. Not every Greek equivalent can therefore be regarded as a 'translation' of the Hebrew word cited. Footnotes draw attention to several cases which fairly certainly represent a Hebrew text different from the MT.

Where LXX references differ from those of the MT, they appear in brackets.

בָּמָה	1 K xi 7 (5)	ὑψηλόν
	Jr xlviii (xxxi) 35	βωμός
	Ezk xx 29	Αβαμα
הַבָּמָה	1 S ix 14, 19	Βαμα
	x 13	βουνός[1]
	1 K iii 4	ὑψηλοτάτη
	2 K xxiii 15	ὑψηλόν
	Is xvi 12	βωμοί

[1] Possibly the LXX is based on a Hebrew text reading הרמה. See also Ps lxxviii (lxxvii) 58.

הַבָּמָה	Ezk xx 29	Αβαμα
מֵהַבָּמָה	1 S ix 25	Βαμα
	x 5	Βαμα
בַּבָּמָה	1 S ix 12	Βαμα
	1 Ch xvi 39	Βαμα
	xxi 29	Βαμα (B: Βαμωθ)
לַבָּמָה	2 Ch i 3	ὑψηλή
	i 13	βαμα
הַבָּמָתָה	1 S ix 13	Βαμα
בָּמוֹת	Nb xxi 19	Βαμωθ
	xxi 28	στῆλαι
	1 K xii 31	ὑψηλά
	xiii 33 (*bis*)	ὑψηλά
	xiv 23	ὑψηλά
	2 K xvii 9, 11, 32	ὑψηλά
	xxiii 8	ὑψηλά
	Jr vii 31	βωμός
	xix 5	ὑψηλά
	xxxii (xxxix) 35	βωμοί
	Ezk xvi 16	εἴδωλα
	Ho x 8	βωμοί
	Am vii 9	βωμοί
	Mi i 5	ἁμαρτία οἴκου (Ιουδα)[1]
	2 Ch xxi 11	ὑψηλά
	xxviii 25	ὑψηλά
	xxxiii 19	ὑψηλά
וּבָתוֹת	Jos xiii 17	Βαμωθβααλ
	Ezk xxxvi 2	ἔρημα
וּמִבָּמוֹת	Nb xxi 20	Βαμωθ
הַבָּמוֹת	1 K xii 32	ὑψηλά
	xiii 2, 32	ὑψηλά
	xxii 44	ὑψηλά
	2 K xii 4	ὑψηλά
	xiv 4	ὑψηλά

[1] Perhaps the LXX is based on a Hebrew text reading ב״ת instead of במות. See also 2 K xxiii 13.

הַבָּמוֹת	2 K xv 4, 35	ὑψηλά
	xvii 29, 32	ὑψηλά
	xviii 4	ὑψηλά
	xxi 3	ὑψηλά
	xxiii 8, 9, 19, 20	ὑψηλά
	xxiii 13	οἶκος[1]
	Is xv 2	βωμός
	2 Ch xiv 4	θυσιαστήριον
	xvii 6	ὑψηλά
	xx 33	ὑψηλά
	xxxi 1	ὑψηλά
	xxxiii 3	ὑψηλά
	xxxiv 3	ὑψηλά
וְהַבָּמוֹת	1 K xv 14	ὑψηλά
	Ezk vi 6	ὑψηλά
	2 Ch xiv 2	ὑψηλά
	xv 17	ὑψηλά
בַּבָּמוֹת	1 K iii 2, 3	ὑψηλά
	xxii 44	ὑψηλά
	2 K xii 4	ὑψηλά
	xiv 4	ὑψηλά
	xv 4, 35	ὑψηλά
	xvi 4	ὑψηλά
	xxiii 5	ὑψηλά
	2 Ch xxviii 4	ὑψηλά
	xxxiii 17	ὑψηλά
לַבָּמוֹת	2 Ch xi 15	ὑψηλά
לְבָמוֹת	Jr xxvi (xxxiii) 18	ἄλσος
	Mi iii 12	ἄλσος
בָּמֳתֵי	Is xiv 14	ἐπάνω[2]
	Am iv 13	ὕψη

1 Perhaps the LXX is based on a Hebrew text reading בית instead of במות. See also Mi i 5.

2 ἐπάνω may only represent על. Possibly the LXX is based on a Hebrew text omitting במתי; alternatively, the LXX translators may have chosen to omit an 'incomprehensible' word (cf. Jb ix 8).

בָּמֳתֵי	Jb ix 8	ἐδάφοι[1]
בָּמֳותֵי[2]	Dt xxxii 13	ἰσχύς
[3]	Is lviii 14	ἀγαθά
[4]	Mi i 3	ὕψη
בָּמוֹתַי	2 S xxii 34	ὕψη
	Hab iii 19	ὑψηλά
בָּמֹתַי	Ps xviii (xvii) 34	ὑψηλά
בָּמוֹתֶיךָ	2 S i 19, 25	ὕψη
בָּמֹתֶיךָ	Jr xvii 3	*LXX omits*
בָּמֹתֵיכֶם	Lv xxvi 30	στήλαι
בָּמוֹתֵיכֶם	Ezk vi 3	ὑψηλά
בָּמֹתָיו	2 K xviii 22	ὑψηλά
	Is xxxvi 7	*Most MSS omit*
	2 Ch xxxii 12	ὑψηλά
בָּמֹתָם	Nb xxxiii 52	στήλαι
בָּמוֹתָם	Ezk xliii 7	ἐν μέσῳ αὐτῶν
בְּבָמוֹתָם	Ps lxxviii (lxxvii) 58	βουνοί[5]
בָּמוֹתֵימוֹ	Dt xxxiii 29	τράχηλος

[1] The LXX is openly paraphrastic here: rendering על־במתי ים by ὡς ἐπ' ἐδάφους ἐπὶ θαλάσσης (cf. Is xiv 14).

[2] Masora Parva: יתיר ו.

[3] *BH*: Q^{MSS} בָּמֳתֵי, K בָּמוֹתֵי.

[4] Masora Parva: במתי ק.

[5] Possibly the LXX is based on a Hebrew text reading ברמותם. See also 1 S x 13